40 DAYS
WITH LABYRINTHS

40 DAYS
WITH LABYRINTHS

Spiritual reflections with labyrinths
to 'walk', colour or decorate

FAY ROWLAND

DARTON·LONGMAN+TODD

First published in 2023 by
Darton, Longman and Todd Ltd
1 Spencer Court
140 – 142 Wandsworth High Street
London SW18 4JJ

© 2023 Fay Rowland

The right of Fay Rowland to be identified as the Author of this work
has been asserted in accordance with the
Copyright, Designs and Patents Act 1988.

ISBN: 978-1-915412-10-2

A catalogue record for this book is available from the British Library.

Designed and produced by Judy Linard

Printed and bound in Great Britain by Short Run Press, Exeter

CONTENTS

INTRODUCTION	7
BREAD	17
Twelve Baskets	18
Whole Food	22
Rock Cakes	26
Moan, Moan, Moan!	30
Elijah and the Angel	34
WALK WITH ME	39
In the Cool of the Day	40
Once Upon a Time	44
Stay With Us	48
A Mixed Multitude	52
A Light on my Path	56
AT HOME	59
Mi Casa es Su Casa	60
In the House of the Lord	64
Picnic on the Beach	68
At Martha and Mary's	72
Staying for Tea	76

WHO IS JESUS? — 81
   Moved into the Neighbourhood — 82
   Who do You Think You Are? — 86
   What About You? — 90
   Peace I Leave with You — 94
   Who are You Looking For? — 98

WATER — 103
   God-Off — 104
   Weeping by the River — 108
   The Rain, it Raineth — 112
   Water Feature — 116
   Anyone Thirsty? — 120

WONDER — 125
   Stardust — 126
   Riding the Wind — 130
   Always with Me — 134
   What are Humans? — 138
   The Heavens Declare — 142

RESTORATION — 147
   I Will Give You Rest — 148
   Pie in the Sky when You Die — 152
   All in the Same Box — 156
   Free Gift — 160
   … As Her Great Love has Shown — 164

FAITH — 169
   How Far? — 170
   But Some Doubted — 174
   Love is … — 178
   Lost and Found — 182
   Aaron's Blessing — 186

INTRODUCTION

Welcome to this book of relaxed Bible devotions with labyrinths. There are forty small chapters, each with a short reading, a reflection and a prayer plus a labyrinth that you can 'walk', colour or decorate.

You may be new to using labyrinths as part of your spiritual life but be assured that they have been a treasured part of Christian spirituality for centuries. The famous Celtic knot designs are a type of labyrinth, and you can find labyrinths in many cathedrals and modern retreat centres as well as hospitals and schools where the benefits of mindfulness are recognised.

A labyrinth is a journey; a long, winding, and often unexpected path. In this, it resembles life with its sudden reversals and inexplicable detours. We can think we are close to our goal only to be turned away. Diversion heaps upon diversion. Then, when we have almost given up hope, the destination opens up before us. We have arrived! Our journey was not the way we'd have planned, and certainly not by the most direct route, but perhaps we've learned something along the way. Perhaps that was the point.

So, come on a labyrinth walk with me along the highways and byways of the Bible, and let's see whom we meet on the path.

BUT I DON'T HAVE A BIBLE!

That's OK. You don't need a Bible to use this book. The Bible passages are printed out, although these are sometimes abbreviated for space. If you want to read the whole passage, Bibles are freely available online through mobile apps and websites such as Bible Gateway. There are translations in almost every language, with a wide choice of English versions: some more scholarly, some more accessible. You can also buy a paper Bible in any good bookshop.

This book uses a variety of translations and you might like to explore which you prefer. I suggest the New International Version (NIV), the Good News Translation (GNT), the New Living Translation (NLT) or The Message, which is an easy-to-read paraphrase. However, unless you have a degree in English Literature, I would not recommend the King James/Authorised Version (KJV/AV). The language is beautifully poetic (it was written in Shakespeare's time) but can be hard to understand and many words have changed their meanings over the last 400 years. Having said that, I've used the KJV for Psalm 23 because it's so darned gorgeous.

You will see references like John 3:16 scattered through this book. These locate texts in the Bible. The word at the start (e.g., John) is the book within the Bible. (The Bible contains 66 books!) These are listed in an index at the front of a paper Bible. The number before the colon (e.g., 3:) is the chapter number, a large number at the start of a paragraph. The last number (e.g., :16) is the verse (a verse is pretty much a sentence) shown by a tiny number within the text. With an online Bible, just type the reference into the search bar, and it will jump to the right place.

Why not try using the references now? Look up John 3:16. It should start, 'For God so loved the world ...'

WHAT IS A LABYRINTH?

Let me clear up a common confusion – labyrinths are different from mazes. This is not a book of puzzles. There are no wrong turns, no dead-ends, no blind alleys or traps. The hand-drawn labyrinths in this book are not designed to trick or confuse you. Instead, they lead you on a journey towards a destination, through winding ways and twisting tracks, but always onwards.

Some are based on ancient designs, dating back to the mists of antiquity, some come from labyrinths found in abbeys or Roman mosaics. Other designs are contemporary and, to the best of my knowledge, unique. Some lead from the outside to the centre, others lead through and emerge at the far side. Some have a long route inwards and a short way out. If you arrive at a centre, you can pause then retrace your steps, or remain in the centre until you have finished your thought process. One advantage of drawn labyrinths is that you can simply close the book and leave without needing to walk all the way back again!

ARE LABYRINTHS FOR ME?

While the most ancient designs predate all major world religions, labyrinths have a long tradition in Christianity as a picture of pilgrimage – a meaningful journey. You can use a labyrinth whether you consider yourself a Christian, any other faith, no faith, or unsure. In the Christian tradition, the path can represent your life journey towards God – not the neat, simple route that we might plan, but full of changes, reversals and the confusion that is common to all. Nevertheless, the path of a labyrinth always, *always* leads the right way.

A labyrinth is an exercise in trust. Often, the path seems to lead away from the centre, not towards, or back to where you've just been. If I walk a labyrinth mown into grass, for example, I might be tempted to step over the 'wall' onto a path that looks more promising. But that will not work. I will either miss part of the journey, repeat sections I have already walked, or even miss the centre completely and find myself back at the entrance.

Perhaps you like to plan everything meticulously in advance. Perhaps you prefer to wing it. Whichever your preference, the truth is that most of the things that are really important in life are not under our control. Sometimes we have to cope with the unexpected or the unwelcome, but life continues.

Walking a labyrinth is a way to explore this and to think through some of life's Big Questions. Martin Luther King put it this way: 'Faith is taking the first step even when you don't see the whole staircase.'

HOW DO I WALK A LABYRINTH?

The short answer is 'However you like.' There is no wrong way to walk a labyrinth, and there is no test at the end of this book to make sure you've done it properly. This is a personal journey for you, and your experience will be different from mine.

However, here are some suggestions that you might find helpful. Feel free to try a selection and don't be afraid to experiment.

Finger walking

Although many labyrinths are huge, constructed of stones with paths wide enough to walk through, others are tiny, fitting on coins. The designs in this book are all finger-sized. Use your finger to 'walk' the path as quickly or slowly as you like. Which fits better with your mood? Where are you on your journey? What do you expect to find at the centre?

Avatar

An avatar is a symbol or icon of something. Look around your room and select a small object that represents yourself, or another person, situation or decision. You might choose a key, a stone, a piece of jewellery or a small ornament. Use the avatar to walk the labyrinth for you, moving it forward in small steps and pausing whenever seems right.

Colour

It's time to get creative! Forget school art lessons. Ignore those nagging voices telling you that you can't draw. Throw away any notion that colouring is for kids. Get out the pens, pencils or paints and bring some life into the lines! As well as being good for your mental wellbeing, colouring is a great way to build some quiet space into your day. The act of colouring grants you head-time while your hands are busy. Think about the Bible passage, talk to God, or just rejoice in the silence.

Some of the labyrinths have paths filled with detailed designs, aching to be coloured. Others have blank paths, which you can fill with your own drawings if you wish. Remember: there is no test at the end of the book. This is between you and God. No one is marking your work. Fill the space with lines, pictures, words or stick men. Make your artwork a prayer, a celebration, a lament or simply a brain dump.

Breath prayers

You can use this in combination with mindful breathing or as a pause when you come to a turn in a labyrinth. Choose a short prayer and repeat the first line as you breathe in, the second line as you breathe out. Allow the words to sink deeply in.

Come / Lord Jesus (Revelation 22:20)
Be still and know / that I am God. (Psalm 46:1)
Be still / before the Lord. (Psalm 37:7)
In returning and rest / is your salvation
in quietness and trust / is your strength. (Isaiah 30:15)

The Lord's Prayer

Alternatively, say The Lord's Prayer one phrase at a time, allowing several breaths for each line and allowing yourself space to think about the meaning of the words. Here are the contemporary and the traditional versions, both based on Jesus' words in Matthew 6, with the 'doxology' (praise) at the end. Use whichever you prefer, or pray it in your first language.

CONTEMPORARY	TRADITIONAL
Our Father in heaven,	Our Father, who art in heaven,
hallowed be your name,	hallowed be thy name;
your kingdom come,	thy kingdom come,
your will be done,	thy will be done
on earth as in heaven.	on earth as it is in heaven.
Give us today our daily bread.	Give us this day our daily bread,
Forgive us our sins	and forgive us our trespasses,
as we forgive those who	as we forgive those who
sin against us.	trespass against us;
Save us from the time of	and lead us not into
trial	temptation,
and deliver us from evil.	but deliver us from evil.
For the kingdom, the power,	For thine is the kingdom,
and the glory are yours	and the power, and the glory,
now and for ever.	for ever and ever.
Amen.	Amen.

Music

Choose some music to play in the background, either instrumental or with lyrics that match the theme. Allow the music to drown out the noises of your busy life and bring your focus to God. Walk slowly through the labyrinth to the rhythm of the music, pausing at the turns until the end of a phrase.

Unloading

Many of us carry around a headful of concerns and worries and a to-do list as long as a gibbon's arm. Use the space around the labyrinth to write down all the loads you are carrying and imagine yourself unpacking a huge rucksack as you do, placing the items on the ground outside the labyrinth as you write them. Then you can walk the labyrinth without the loads.

Don't worry, you have not lost them. If you need to, you can pick them up on your way out and put them back in your pack. But perhaps you might not take all of them.

Candle

You can use a candle as a focus while you are walking your labyrinth to symbolise Jesus, the Light of the World. The smoke rising can remind us of our prayers rising to God. You can say this prayer when you light your candle.

Jesus said, 'I am the light of the world. Whoever follows me will never walk in darkness, but will have the light of life.' (John 8:12) Lord Jesus, be my light as I walk. Amen.

Holy ground

The Old Testament tells how Moses met God by a flaming bush. 'Take off your sandals,' said God, 'for this is holy ground.'

When I walk a full-sized labyrinth, I walk barefoot when practical. There is something about removing my shoes that reminds me that I am in a special place. You can do the same with these finger labyrinths, removing your footwear before you enter. Leave your cares and worries at the entrance alongside your shoes and socks. They will be waiting for you when you return, although perhaps a little altered.

Silence
The Bible tells the story of Elijah meeting God not in the crashing storm, not in the mighty earthquake, not in the roaring fire but after the fire, in the sound of utter silence. (You can find this in I Kings 19.) Such silence can be hard to find in our modern world, filled with Google and Netflix, e-everything and i-everything else.

One way to bring our attention inwards, away from the distractions around is to use a 5-4-3-2-1. This won't make the noises go away but can help you to adjust your focus.

> Start by looking out of a window. Notice five things you can see or hear. Next focus on the building you are in. Count four things that are happening in other rooms. Now bring your vision into your room. Look around and notice three things that could distract you. Consciously lay them aside. They are not your focus at present. Then close your eyes and concentrate on your body. Note two things that you are touching. Finally, look deeper inside and see the one soul that is you, calm and ready to hear God's voice.

Mindful breathing
If your mind is racing with all thing things you have to do, you can use the labyrinths as an excuse to slow down for a few minutes. Sit comfortably, with your feet flat on the floor and your hands in your lap.

Close your eyes and imagine a large square in front of you. Start in a lower corner and breath in as you travel up the side. Hold the breath as you move along the top of the square and release the breath as you travel down the other side. Pause, moving along the bottom of the square and then start again. This will slow your breathing, stilling your soul to hear God.

When you feel ready, turn your hands palm up, bringing to God what is on your heart and ready to receive. Then enter the labyrinth with a short prayer.

Lord Jesus, I breathe out my concerns and breathe in your peace. Amen.

Conflict

If you have a conflict to work through, choose a labyrinth that has two equal paths to the centre: one for each of you. Use the circuits to think about the disagreement in a calm and balanced manner. As each party moves around the first circuit, state in simple terms what you understand the problem to be, remembering to use 'I think …' or 'I feel …' statements, not 'You this' or 'You that'.

In the second circuit, restate what you have heard the other party say and acknowledge that they have the right to feel that way, even if you feel differently. In the remaining circuits, suggest ways that the conflict could be resolved or moved forwards and make some agreement, however small, as you meet in the middle.

BREAD

Bread – whether gluten-free, multigrain sliced or sundried tomato focaccia – is important. It's a metaphor for the essentials of life. The job that pays your rent is your bread and butter; you realise what's important when you know which side your bread is buttered; and a brilliant invention is the best thing since sliced bread. Even The Lord's Prayer says, 'give us today our daily bread'.

So here is a collection of readings about bread. Mine's a crusty bloomer with low-fat spread, please.

TWELVE BASKETS

READING

When it was evening, his followers came to him and said, 'No one lives in this place, and it is already late. Send the people away so they can go to the towns and buy food for themselves.'

But Jesus answered, 'They don't need to go away. You give them something to eat.'

They said to him, 'But we have only five loaves of bread and two fish.'

Jesus said, 'Bring the bread and the fish to me.' Then he told the people to sit down on the grass. He took the five loaves and the two fish and, looking to heaven, he thanked God for the food. Jesus divided the bread and gave it to his followers, who gave it to the people. All the people ate and were satisfied. Then the followers filled twelve baskets with the leftover pieces of food. There were about five thousand men there who ate, not counting women and children.

(Matthew 14:15-21 NCV)

THINKING

A long time ago, in a galaxy far, far away there was a pandemic, and some people hoarded loo rolls. Why did they do that? Blame our prehistoric brains. When there might not be enough of something, our brains tell us to keep what there is for ourselves. Hopefully our more modern altruism circuits cut in and say 'Share!', but fear can make us do weird things.

I wonder if there was the *teeniest* bit of prehistoric brain going on with the disciples in this story. Jesus talked to the crowd as morning became afternoon and passed into teatime. I can imagine the disciples lounging on the grass around Jesus, listening to the crowd's rumbling stomachs and waiting for an ad break.

The disciples had their food sorted already. They'd sent Thomas to the takeaway in the village. He came back with twelve orders of chicken burgers and chips. Peter counted the steaming hot baskets. 'Didn't you get one for Jesus?' he asked.

'Oh, I didn't think of that,' said Thomas, red-faced. 'My nephew here's got some sardine sandwiches. We could give him those. And we could divvy up the chips, perhaps?'

'But then I won't have enough,' Peter growled. 'And you know what Jesus is like. If we offer him food, he'll want to feed the whole bloomin' crowd as well.' He glanced round at the other disciples and lowered his voice. 'We should just scoff this quickly. He'll never notice.'

We know what happened next. A lad's lunch feeds twenty thousand, and the disciples learn that giving to God does not lessen what we have but transforms it beyond our imagination.

I wonder what I am clutching tightly for fear of losing it if I give it to God. I wonder what might happen if I loosen my grip.

(The bit about chicken burgers is made up. But you have to wonder where they got twelve baskets from, eh?)

RESPONDING

Lord Father,
It seems logical that the more I give to you
the less I have for myself,
but perhaps ...
Perhaps your kingdom doesn't work like that.
Perhaps when I give I don't lose, but gain.
Perhaps.
Amen.

EXPLORING FURTHER

In Matthew's gospel, this episode is sandwiched (do you see what I did there?) between the sad story of the execution of John the Baptist, Jesus' cousin, and Jesus calling Peter to literally step out of his comfort zone. You can read about all of these in Matthew 14.

WALKING

Take a few moments to still your mind (you can find some suggestions in the 'How do I walk a labyrinth' section), then walk through the simple labyrinth on page 18. The path is not complicated, but there is much to look at along the way. Slow your journey. What do you notice?

WHOLE FOOD

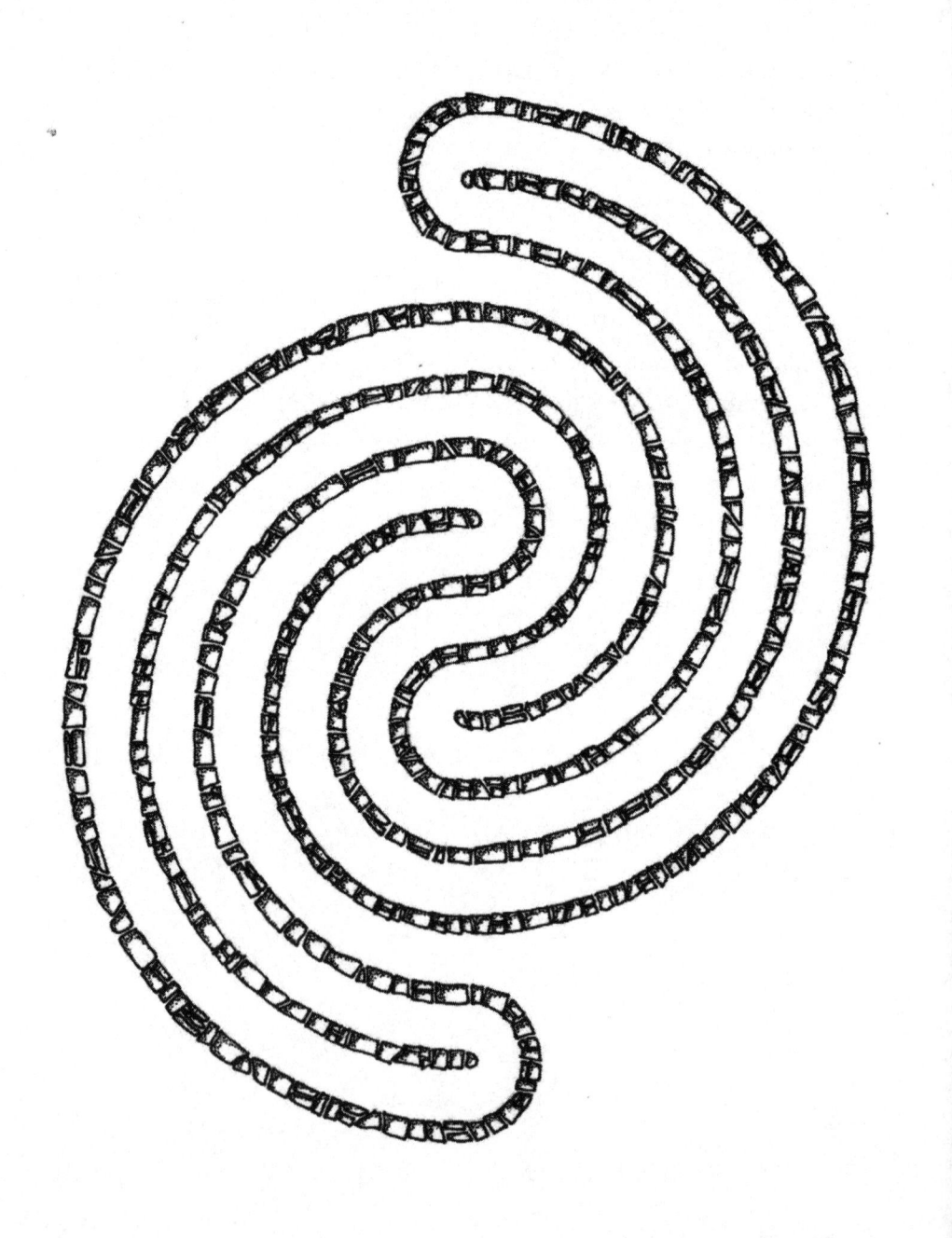

READING

Jesus said, 'I tell you the truth. Moses was not the one who gave you bread from heaven. But my Father gives you the true bread from heaven. God's bread is the One who comes down from heaven and gives life to the world.'

The people said, 'Sir, give us this bread always.'

Then Jesus said, 'I am the bread that gives life. He who comes to me will never be hungry. He who believes in me will never be thirsty.'

(John 6:32-35 ICB)

THINKING

I recently got caught by the trolley police. You know, the ones who scan your shopping cart and make you feel guilty if it's full of unhealthy food. Mine was bulging with mini-pizzas, cheesy twists and iced buns. I explained that I was buying goodies for a birthday lunch and they let me off with a warning. Note to self: next time, put a lettuce on top of the treats.

OK, tenuous link. I bought bread-based foodstuffs and Jesus described himself as the Bread of Life.

Other cultures have different mealtime must-haves. For the Israelites of Jesus' time, it was bread. For Koreans, it's kimchi. (Fun fact: the first Korean aboard the International Space Station had 'space kimchi' flown up specially.) If Jesus has lived in Ireland he might have said, 'I am the potato of life.' In Japan, 'I am the ramen noodle of life.' Or perhaps not. It doesn't quite have the same ring to it.

Centuries ago, a guy called Augustine wondered about the must-haves of life. He'd tried the lot – money, sex, power – he lived in the fast lane and rose rapidly to the top of his profession. But there was something more, and Augustine realised that he was missing life's must-haves.

Torn between meaningless pleasure and the deeper, richer life he knew was lacking, Augustine prayed the famously honest, 'Lord, give me chastity and continency, only not yet.' God must have chuckled at that.

Eventually Augustine gave in. His life had been pizza without the mozzarella, chips without the salt, pot noodle without the little sachet of monosodium glutamate. It was tasteless and unsatisfying. He recognised in himself what mathematician and theologian Blaise Pascal would later describe as a 'God-shaped hole', which nothing else would fill. Augustine put it like this, 'You have made us for yourself, O Lord, and our hearts are restless until they rest in You.'

For both Pascal and Augustine, their must-have turned out to be Jesus, the Bread of Life.

RESPONDING

Lord Father,
You have made me for yourself, and my heart is restless.
I try to quell that restlessness with padding,
and it works, for a while.
But I'm only dulling my hunger
with sweets and candy floss.
And I know that, really.
Amen.

EXPLORING FURTHER

This 'bread from heaven' that the people were talking about dates from Moses' time. We'll look at that in a later chapter, but if you want to read about it now, look in Exodus 16.

WALKING

The spiral labyrinth above reflects Augustine's restless heart, switching back and forth. As you enter, allow your mind to calm and train your ears to hear God's voice. What is bread for you? Where do you spend your time, your energy? Are you happy with that, or would you like different things to be important?

ROCK CAKES

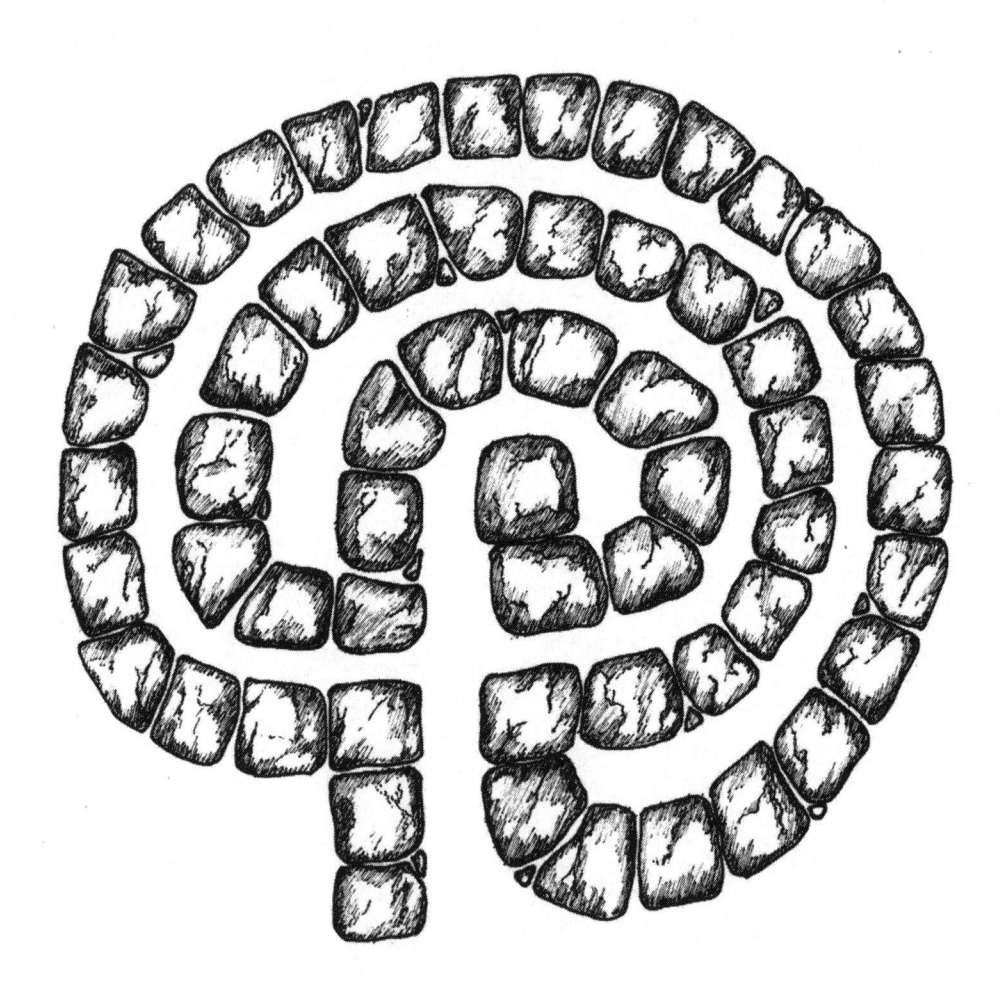

READING

Then Jesus was led by the Spirit into the wilderness to be tempted by the devil. After fasting for forty days and forty nights, he was hungry. The tempter came to him and said, 'If you are the Son of God, tell these stones to become bread.'

Jesus answered, 'It is written: 'Man shall not live on bread alone, but on every word that comes from the mouth of God.'

(Matthew 4:1-4 NIV)

THINKING

I'm a fraud.

There. I've said it. The dreadful secret I've been hiding all my life. Those things I'm supposed to be good at? I'm not. And one day, I'll get found out. Someone will whisper over my shoulder, '*If* you are good at your job why weren't you promoted?' '*If* you are so clever why did you get that wrong, eh?' And I won't have anything to say. I'll crawl into a hole and drink a mug of self-pity, with three sugars.

Anyone else suffer from imposter syndrome? No? Just me then.

Except it's all lies. Worth is not defined by money or sales or social media 'likes'. There are plenty of brilliant musicians who have not sold a million records, plenty of talented artists whose work is not hanging in the Tate, plenty of gifted footballers who will never get signed for Liverpool. Those whispering doubts? They're lies.

Jesus heard those whispers too. '*If* you are the son of God, tell these stones to become bread.' If. If. If. But Jesus had a comeback. 'Bread is not important. Neither are miracles. They don't define me. I know who I am because of what God says.'

Jesus changed the focus. He moved it away from status and possessions, doing tricks to impress people, and towards his relationship with God. God's word was like bread to him, the food that fed him day by day. And the tempter had no answer. He slunk away with a mug of self-pity. No sugar.

God says I am loved. I'm not perfect, got plenty of work to do yet, but loved, ultimately loved. Why? Because I'm 'all that'? No. Because God is nice. What a relief! I don't have to live up to a fake image of perfection, and I can quit beating myself up because I fail.

So I think I might take Jesus' advice. I'll listen to God's opinion of me, not those whispering voices that tell me I'm no good. Nor will I listen to the flattering pride that tells me I'm utterly brilliant.

I'll have bread for lunch today.

RESPONDING

Loving Lord,
Please help me to get a right image
of who I am in your sight.
To realise that you love me
because you love me
because you love me.
And that is all.
Amen.

EXPLORING FURTHER

This event was right at the start of Jesus' ministry. He was about 30 years old when he started gathering his group of disciples and teaching about God's kingdom. You can read about it in the rest of Matthew 4.

WALKING

This stepping-stone labyrinth is an ancient design, dating from several centuries before Jesus. As you step from rock to rock, imagine each becoming bread for your soul, God's word to you. What is God saying to you today?

MOAN, MOAN, MOAN!

READING

In the desert, the whole community grumbled against Moses and Aaron. The Israelites said to them, 'If only we had died by the Lord's hand in Egypt! There we sat round pots of meat and ate all the food we wanted, but you have brought us out into this desert to starve this entire assembly to death.'

The Lord said to Moses, 'I have heard the grumbling of the Israelites. Tell them, 'At twilight, you will eat meat, and in the morning, you will be filled with bread. Then you will know that I am the Lord your God.'

(Exodus 16:2-3, 11-12 NIV)

THINKING

A toddler is lying on the floor, red of face and hearty of lung, arms and legs flailing. The reason for this tiny tumult of fury? He wanted milk on his cereals but didn't want his cereals to get wet. True story. The internet is littered with photos of raging tots captioned by their puzzled parents: 'She wanted a jam sandwich. I gave her a jam sandwich. Apparently, I am a monster.'

As one who has weathered the stormy 'terrible twos', I can verify that The Wrath of Kahn is nothing compared to that of a frustrated toddler. Milk, a warm blanket and a hug often help. (They're good for the tot as well!)

I imagine God listening to the moaning Israelites with the same look of bewildered weariness on his face. 'They asked to be rescued. I rescued them. Now they're complaining about being rescued!' Honestly, there's no pleasing some people. (Fun fact: those 'pots of meat' that they supposedly sat around while slaves in Egypt are where we get our 'fleshpots' from.)

Fast forward to almost any point in the next forty years and you'll hear God's children throwing toddler-like tantrums at every little thing. So God sighs, picks up his wailing child (who wipes a snotty nose on his shoulder), and chops the jam sandwiches into triangles instead of squares because they taste different like that. Then they settle on the sofa with a blanket. Contentment. Until the next tantrum.

Of course, as a mature, well-balanced adult, I am nothing like the stroppy toddler. I'd never ask God to make me more patient and then complain about that irritating person who gets on my nerves. Or pray, '… as we forgive those who …' and then whinge about someone who has wronged me. I meant that God should zap me with forgiveness, not make me learn it for myself.

Nope. Nothing like the toddler at all.

RESPONDING

> Loving Father God,
> compassionate and gracious,
> slow to anger, swift to forgive
> and full to the brim with love and faithfulness,
> you are more patient with me than I deserve,
> and more kind than I can imagine.
> Thank you.
> Amen.

EXPLORING FURTHER

This wasn't the only time that these newly-freed Israelite slaves complained about their rescue. I've abbreviated the story a lot, but you can read the whole thing in Exodus 16, then flip over the page to Exodus 17 to read the next lot of complaining.

WALKING

This labyrinth is based on a design found in 1914 carved into a rock in California and thought to be over 2,000 years old. The design is unique to the Americas, and is unusual in that it goes precisely nowhere! Start at the centre and follow the path to arrive adjacent to where you started. How annoying. The Israelites must have felt a similar frustration as they wandered in the desert between Egypt and Israel. What was God teaching them? What is God teaching you?

ELIJAH AND THE ANGEL

READING

When Elijah saw how things were, he ran for dear life to Beersheba, far in the south of Judah. He left his young servant there and then went on into the desert another day's journey. He came to a lone broom bush and collapsed in its shade, wanting in the worst way to be done with it all—to just die: 'Enough of this, God! Take my life—I'm ready to join my ancestors in the grave!' Exhausted, he fell asleep under the lone broom bush.

Suddenly an angel shook him awake and said, 'Get up and eat!'

He looked around and, to his surprise, right by his head were a loaf of bread baked on some coals and a jug of water. He ate the meal and went back to sleep.

(1 Kings 19:3-6 MSG)

THINKING

Elijah was a big man.

I don't mean he was 6' 8' and built like a brick privy. I mean he was a big personality, a celeb before celebs were a thing. He was a trailblazer, an activist, idealistic, principled, ready to right the wrongs of the world. Think of that guy in Tiananmen Square facing down the tank. That's Elijah. But speaking the truth to power can be dangerous, and Elijah was on the run for his life. As we meet him, he is physically, mentally and spiritually worn out, and he turns to God.

Notice what God *didn't* do. He didn't send an angel to say, 'Pull yourself together, man! Stop being so miserable.' Never, in the history of telling someone to stop being miserable, has that ever stopped them from being miserable.

Instead, God gave Elijah space and rest and food, and when Elijah felt able, God took him to a high mountain, the one on which Moses had stood centuries before, and listened as Elijah unburdened his heart.

It's OK to tell God how we feel. He knows anyway, so we don't have to put on our Sunday smiles and pretend that everything is fine when it's not. God knows when we yelled at someone because we were worried about something else. God knows that the million gnat-bites of daily stress eventually become too much and we need to hide under the blankets for a while. God also knows that sometimes we need more help, and that's fine. God gave us medical professionals who can help with hurting heads and well as hurting hamstrings.

But, while God meets us where we are, he does not leave us where we are. God did not ignore Elijah's worries and woes, but he did not leave Elijah to wallow in them either. Instead, he gave him a path out of his pit and way forward, when Elijah was ready.

RESPONDING

God,
thank you that you know me,
the real 'me' that I don't show to people
because they might think I'm stupid.
Thank you that you know my darkest self-doubts,
my impossible dreams, my heart-break longings.
It is good to be known.
Amen.

EXPLORING FURTHER

We'll look at the bust-up that had Elijah running for his life in another chapter (God-Off), but if you want to read it now, it's in 1 Kings 18. You can find out how God helped Elijah through his down in the rest of 1 Kings 19.

WALKING

Elijah had a lot on his mind, understandably so. What mental burdens are you carrying? As you walk this labyrinth, imagine laying one item down at each turn, naming them before God. You might like to draw or write them along the path. Reach the centre unburdened and commit the items to God's care.

WALK WITH ME

Walking is a companionable activity – not the stress of a race, but still moving onwards. It is an exercise that is easy on aching joints and soothing for the soul, walking in the company of others or in the company of your own thoughts.

Jesus often walked with his disciples, teaching them as they ambled together through life, and one of his most famous stories-with-a-point starts with a walk: 'A man went down from Jerusalem to Jericho …'

Why not come on a walk with me and let's see where we end up.

IN THE COOL OF THE DAY

READING

Then they [Adam and Eve] heard the Lord God walking in the garden during the cool part of the day, and the man and his wife hid from the Lord God among the trees in the garden. But the Lord God called to the man and said, 'Where are you?'

The man answered, 'I heard you walking in the garden, and I was afraid because I was naked, so I hid.'

(Genesis 3:8-10 NCV)

THINKING

This is one of the most beautiful and yet one of the saddest parts of the Bible. It's a story that describes how humans and God got separated. A couple of chapters earlier, we read how God created humans in his own image, and it was very good. They lived together in this picture-perfect world – Eden – walking in the garden in the cool of the day.

It conjures up pictures of a lazy summer's evening, walking home after a picnic. There's a loopy hound bouncing around after butterflies and just enough cloud to make the low sun look picturesque. I can remember evenings like that from my childhood, although I'm sure that the years have painted them rosier than reality.

But there's something wrong with this picture. God is walking alone. The people are hiding. Why aren't they walking with God anymore?

Another childhood memory. We had a spaniel called Meg, and one day I came home from school to find her cowering under the table, shaking and whimpering. Why?

Guilt.

On the table was mum's freshly-baked sponge cake. Well, half of it. The rest was inside Meg. She knew she had done wrong and deserved a telling-off. She got one, and was sent to her basket, and then she was fine.

So what of God and us? Does God send us to our baskets? No, God is in the business of reconciliation, not punishment. But just like with Meg, when guilt is gnawing inside, it needs dealing with. Unresolved guilt festers and poisons. That's why the humans hid from God and why God, in kindness, took them from Eden until they could be restored and return to walk with him in the garden – the picture we see right at the end of the Bible.

In the meantime, we can find forgiveness in Jesus, no matter what we feel bad about. Restoration is freely available to all. No sending to baskets needed.

RESPONDING

God of mercy,
We both know that I do things wrong.
Some are innocent mistakes,
some are accidents that I cannot help.
But some are deliberate,
and in the small hours of the night
I feel guilt grinding at my soul.
Please forgive me and make me new.
So that I may walk in the garden in the cool of the day,
at your side.
Amen.

EXPLORING FURTHER

In Genesis 3, the humans were banished from Eden to stop them eating from the Tree of Life and living forever in their broken state. But flick to the opposite end of the Bible to read how it all turns out. Revelation 22 shows a picture of heaven, the Tree of Life bridging a river of living water and bringing healing and redemption to all.

WALKING

Enter this leafy labyrinth at the left side of the trunk and amble through the garden in the cool of the day until you reach the centre. Stay a while, enjoying the rustle of the leaves and the song of the birds, then depart in peace on the other side of the trunk. Where will you take that peace today?

ONCE UPON A TIME

READING

The man wanted to justify his lack of love for some kinds of people, so he asked, 'Which neighbours?'

Jesus replied with an illustration: 'A Jew going on a trip from Jerusalem to Jericho was attacked by bandits. They stripped him of his clothes and money, and beat him up and left him lying half dead beside the road.

'By chance a Jewish priest came along; and when he saw the man lying there, he crossed to the other side of the road and passed him by. A Jewish Temple-assistant walked over and looked at him lying there, but then went on.

'But a despised Samaritan came along, and when he saw him, he felt deep pity. Kneeling beside him the Samaritan soothed his wounds with medicine and bandaged them. Then he put the man on his donkey and walked along beside him till they came to an inn, where he nursed him through the night. The next day he handed the innkeeper two twenty-dollar bills and told him to take care of the man. "If his bill runs higher than that," he said, "I'll pay the difference the next time I am here."

'Now which of these three would you say was a neighbour to the bandits' victim?'

The man replied, 'The one who showed him some pity.'

Then Jesus said, 'Yes, now go and do the same.'

(Luke 10:29-37 TLB)

THINKING

The Good Samaritan is probably Jesus' most famous story, but we often miss the real impact because of our culture. It's not a story about helping people, although that's good, of course. It's about seeing others through God's eyes.

A man asked Jesus how to live a good life. 'What do you think?' Jesus replied.

'Love God with everything you have, and love your neighbour as yourself,' said the man.

'Good answer,' said Jesus.

'Yeah, but ...' the man squirmed, 'but who is my neighbour?' (hoping it meant people like him). So Jesus told a story about a Samaritan.

These days, Samaritans are good people who talk you down off a bridge, but not so in Jesus' day. Samaritans were the Israelites' traditional enemy: Darth Vader to their Obi-wan Kenobi, Voldemort to their Harry. So the idea that this flea-ridden, fart-sniffing snot rag could teach the priest or the Levite how to please God was ... explosive! It would be like Richard Dawkins teaching the Pope how to be Catholic!

Jesus was trying to expand the man's idea of who could be in God's family. Sure, the 'nice' people with clean fingernails and polished cars. But also the grubby folks, the ones who can't sit still, the ones who aren't sure what they believe, the ones with problems in their pasts, the ones with problems in their futures, and yes, the flea-ridden, fart-sniffing Samaritans.

RESPONDING

Loving Lord,
I know that you love everyone
and you want me to do the same.
But, if I'm honest, I don't always want to.

Please help me to see others with your eyes
and to love them as you love me.
Amen.

EXPLORING FURTHER

Matthew 9 tells of Jesus befriending all kinds of 'unsuitable' people and Acts 10, which is set after the first Easter, describes how the new (Jewish) Christians learn that God accepts people of every nation into his family. Who are today's 'unsuitable' people?

WALKING

I imagine that the man in this story must have been very confused when he woke up in the inn – not just from the beating and the strange room, but from the news that his rescuer had been a Samaritan. It can be disorienting when we have the change our ideas about people. Walk this stumbling labyrinth and pause at the turns to think about which ideas you might need to change.

STAY WITH US

READING

That same day two of Jesus' followers were going to a town named Emmaus, about seven miles from Jerusalem. They were talking about everything that had happened. While they were talking and discussing, Jesus himself came near and began walking with them, but they were kept from recognizing him.

They came near the town of Emmaus, and Jesus acted as if he were going farther. But they begged him, 'Stay with us, because it is late; it is almost night.' So he went in to stay with them.

(Luke 24:13-16, 28-29 NCV)

THINKING

It is the evening of the first Easter Sunday. After the trauma of Good Friday, the tortuous waiting of Saturday and the bewildering news of Sunday morning, two disciples are walking home, trying to make sense of it all.

And Jesus comes and walks with them. This reminds me of the story in Genesis (see 'In the cool of the day') where God wants to walk with the people in the garden, but they hide. Now, with restoration freely offered to all, God in Jesus walks with his children in the cool of the day.

They walk and talk until they are almost at the town, and the disciples don't want this soothing stranger to leave. 'Stay with us,' they beg, and he does. As Jesus breaks bread that evening, something clears in their minds and they recognise him. Perhaps they remembered the Last Supper. Perhaps they were part of the crowd fed with five loaves and two fish. Perhaps it just needed time to sink in. Some *thinks* take time.

I can be like that too. I can read a bit of Bible that I've read a hundred times before and suddenly – Pow! – the words hurtle off the page and catch me a swift right hook and I wonder how I managed to not see that for so long. Some *thinks* take time.

I love how patient Jesus was with these confused followers of his. Did he tell them off because their theology was not correct? Did he say they should come back when they could explain the Trinity? No. Jesus walked alongside them, and hoped that they'd invite him to stay.

Of course, it's fine to ask questions, it's good to learn about what we believe – a faith that does not stand up to scrutiny is little better than superstition – but what really matters is walking with Jesus, and inviting him to stay.

RESPONDING

Loving Lord Jesus,
You are greater than our minds,
yet we may know you.
You are beyond comprehension,
yet we may recognise you.
Come, Lord Jesus, and stay with us.
Amen.

EXPLORING FURTHER

The extract above is only a tiny part of this beautiful story. You'll find the whole episode in Luke 24.

WALKING

This simple labyrinth reminds me of the tiling patterns found in some homes of Biblical times. Imagine that they are in your home, and you are inviting Jesus to stay. How would you welcome Jesus?

A MIXED MULTITUDE

READING

The Israelites travelled from Rameses to Succoth. There were about six hundred thousand men walking, not including the women and children. Many other people who were not Israelites went with them, as well as a large number of sheep, goats, and cattle.

(Exodus 12:37-38 NCV)

THINKING

Exodus - the central event in Jewish history and it gets a whole book of the Bible named after it. The Israelites were slaves in Egypt. Moses has a huge argy-bargy with Pharoah Rameses II, with plagues of boils and frogs and what have you, and Pharoah (eventually) chases them out like an angry farmer brandishing a pitchfork and yelling, 'Get off my land!'

So we meet these newly-freed slaves at the start of a long journey back home. But have you noticed who left? It wasn't just the Israelites. There were maybe two million of them plus their flocks and herds, but also *many other people.* A mixed multitude. A rag-tag rabble of misfits, none of whom knew where they were going or how to get there. (Fun fact: it wasn't actually that far a journey. It would have taken 12 days to get Israel out of Egypt, but it needed 40 years to get Egypt out of Israel.)

And here's the bit that warms my heart. After this, when God talks to his children, they are the Israelites and the *foreigners who live among them.* These strangers are adopted into God's family, part of the covenant. Some of them even end up as Jesus' ancestors!

So what does that have to do with me? I'm not an escaping

Egyptian slave. True, but this is about being an 'inny' or an 'outy' – and I'm not talking belly buttons.

We all have groups that we feel we're 'in' or not. It can be hurtful if we find that we are out of some group that we think we should be in. Or perhaps we're in a group but don't feel secure, thinking, 'How long before someone spots that I don't belong here and boots me out?'

I have good news for you. God's people have always been, let us say, a bit pick-and-mix. Every family has some weirdos, and God's is no exception. Whether you're a zany cousin Zak or a strait-laced Aunty Stella, there is a place for you at God's table.

Of course, God's children are human and we get things wrong. So if we feel like we're insiders, let's make sure our gatherings reflect God's inclusive welcome of all. And if we feel like outsiders, let's hear God's warm welcome into his gloriously oddball 'mixed multitude'.

RESPONDING

Loving Lord Jesus,
Thank you that no matter what my background,
no matter what my nationality,
no matter what my gender, status, colour, size or age,
I can be part of your mixed multitude.
Amen.

EXPLORING FURTHER

Towards the end of his life, Moses reminded the Israelites of God's care for them and the foreigners who lived among them. You can read it in Deuteronomy 10, especially from verse 12.

WALKING

The people who left Egypt had a lot of spiritual rubbish to get rid of along the way. As you walk this labyrinth, a design often seen in Roman mosaics, notice the scattered rubbish along the path. Ask God what rubbish you need to leave behind, and ask him to help you.

A LIGHT ON MY PATH

READING

Your word is a lamp for my feet, a light on my path.

(Psalm 119:105 NIV)

THINKING

I love to drive along flower-edged country roads on a summer's day: rolling hills, cute villages, maybe even a duck pond, and a tower in the distance to mark my destination.

The same journey at night is not so great. I can see nothing beyond my headlights, less than that if it's foggy. I'm fearful of meeting a lorry around every bend and I can't see where I'm headed. It's unsettling and stressful. Kinda like life.

One way to avoid the worries of life is to know everything in advance, then I could avoid all the potholes that I see now through my rear-view mirror. But I'm not sure that I'd want a blueprint of my entire existence, with every detail mapped out in advance, even if that were possible. A life cast in concrete sounds both boring and terrifying at the same time!

The psalm writer had the right idea. He was thinking about how God's word was like a guiding lamp for his feet. Not the entire route map. But enough to see the next few steps.

Jesus gave the same advice to his disciples. 'Do not worry about tomorrow, for tomorrow will worry about itself. Each day has enough trouble of its own.' (Matthew 6:34 NIV)

Car headlights might not be much good on a foggy night, but when it comes to driving through life, God's route-planning is far better than any sat nav. Guidance for the next step, recalculating when we stray off course, and bringing us to our ultimate destination. So I don't need to get bogged down in what might or might not happen in five years. Right now is enough to think about. I'll leave the rest in God's care.

RESPONDING

> Loving Lord,
> Part of me wants to control my life,
> part of me knows I never can,
> not the things that really matter.
> All I have is the part of the path I can see
> and your word to guide me.
> Help me to trust you and walk with you,
> starting today.
> Amen.

EXPLORING FURTHER

Psalm 119 is the longest chapter in the whole Bible. For something shorter on a similar theme, have a look at Proverbs 3:1-6 for kindly wisdom written by Solomon for his son. (Spoiler: son didn't take the advice. Nothing changes.)

WALKING

This labyrinth has some areas that are light, some dark and some between. Where do you feel you are at the moment? Start in the central area that matches this and follow the path through the changes of life, asking God to guide your steps as you go.

AT HOME

Home is important. It does not have to be big or fancy or posh, but it does need to be safe. Home is a place where you can be yourself, where you can be known as you are and accepted. No need for a mask, no need for make-up, no need to impress. At home you can dress like a slob and no one will mind.

God talks about home all through the Bible, promising that his home has rooms enough for us all, and welcoming even the loneliest outcast into his family. Join me in a tour of God's home.

MI CASA ES SU CASA

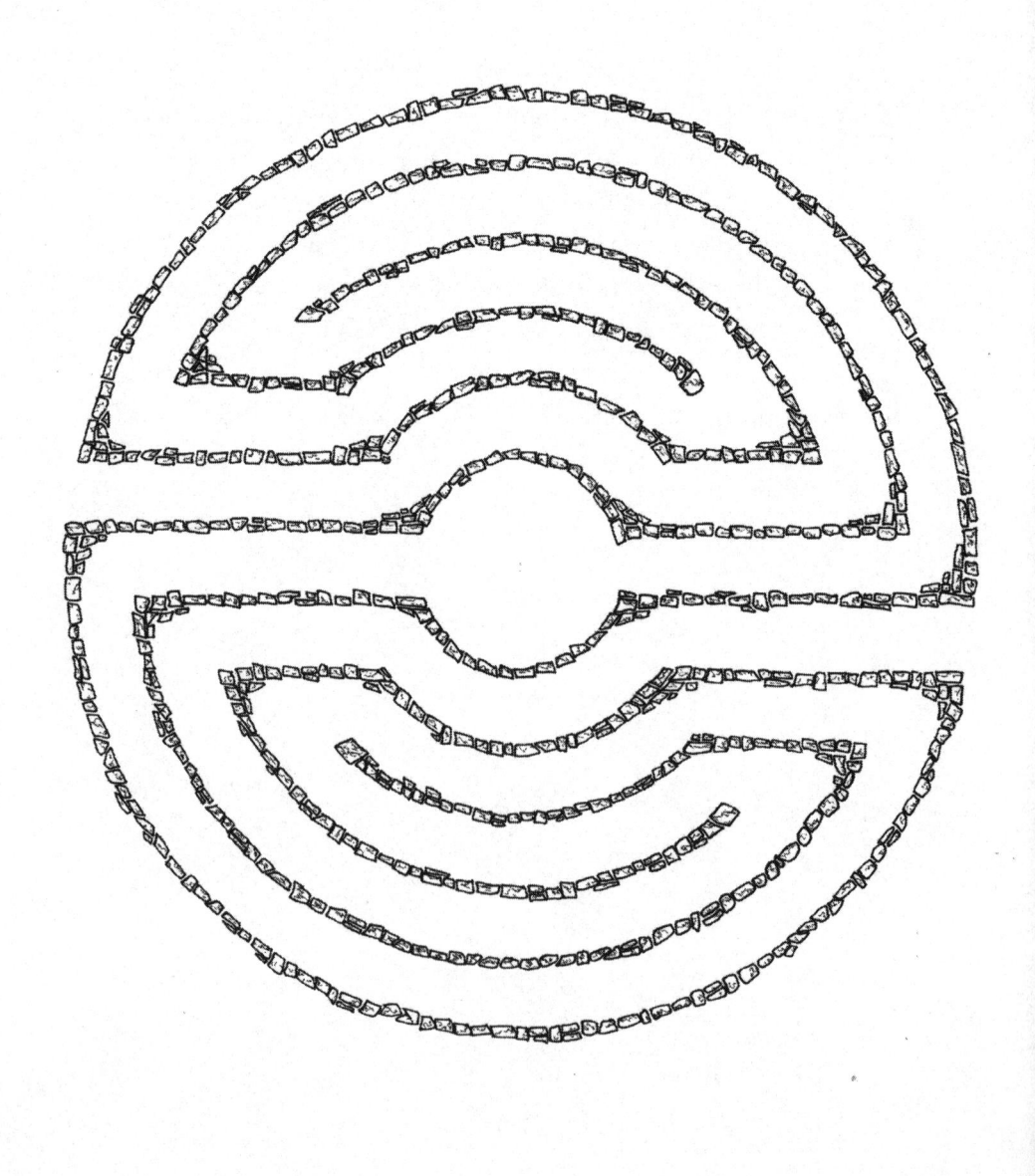

READING

But Ruth replied, 'Don't ask me to leave you and turn back. Wherever you go, I will go; wherever you live, I will live. Your people will be my people, and your God will be my God.

(Ruth 1:16 NLT)

THINKING

Who doesn't love a good romance? Hollywood has made millions from setting hearts a-flutter and the Bible has a rom-com cracker in the story of Ruth.

The scene opens on an Israelite family walking to neighbouring Moab to escape a famine. They settle, the sons grow and marry, and all is well. But then – disaster! – the father dies and the sons, leaving elderly matriarch, Naomi, weeping at their gravesides. Cue the sad music.

Tears still wet on her face, Naomi sets off toward her homeland. But who is this, pelting down the road after her, cloak and bag flying? Why, it is her daughter-in-law, Ruth. 'I'm coming with you,' she calls, holding her bonnet on with one hand.

Sorry, forget the bonnet. I went all Jane Austen for a moment.

Then Naomi tries to dissuade Ruth, 'You're young. Go back and marry again.' But Ruth insists and they travel to Naomi's hometown where Ruth gets a minimum-wage job picking crops. Crops that *just happen* to be owned by the rich and handsome Boaz, a relative of Naomi and probably played by Colin Firth. You can guess the rest. In true Hollywood style, there is a last-minute twist, but it all ends happily. Pass the tissues.

Lovely, but why is that in the Bible?

Well, apart from showing that God loves a rom-com as much as anyone, this little verse gives us the clue: 'Your people shall be my people, and your God shall be my God.' Ruth wanted to be part of Naomi's family and Naomi's faith. Would Naomi's relatives accept her? She didn't talk like them or dress like them. She was the misfit, like asking for Yorkshire tea in a Lancashire cafe. No problem with God's family, however. God's children have always been a mixed bunch, and Ruth fitted right in.

The film ends as Ruth marries Boaz and they settle in Bethlehem (as in 'O Little Town of …'), where they have a son who has a son who has a son called David, (as in 'Once in Royal David's City')..Yes, *that* David. And *he* was the ancestor of Jesus. How's that for a happy ending?

RESPONDING

> Loving Father,
> Thank you that you welcomed Ruth into your family.
> Thank you that your home is big enough for all who come to you.
> Thank you that your arms are wide enough to embrace even me.
> Amen.

EXPLORING FURTHER

Ruth is a short book, only four chapters, so why not get a cup of tea and a couple of chocolate biscuits and read the whole story of our plucky heroine and the God she loved?

WALKING

This labyrinth can either be used to show a journey – into the centre, then outwards to a different place – or a meeting, with two parties starting opposite each other and coming together in the centre. Which of these is more relevant to you right now? Where will you see God along the way?

IN THE HOUSE OF THE LORD

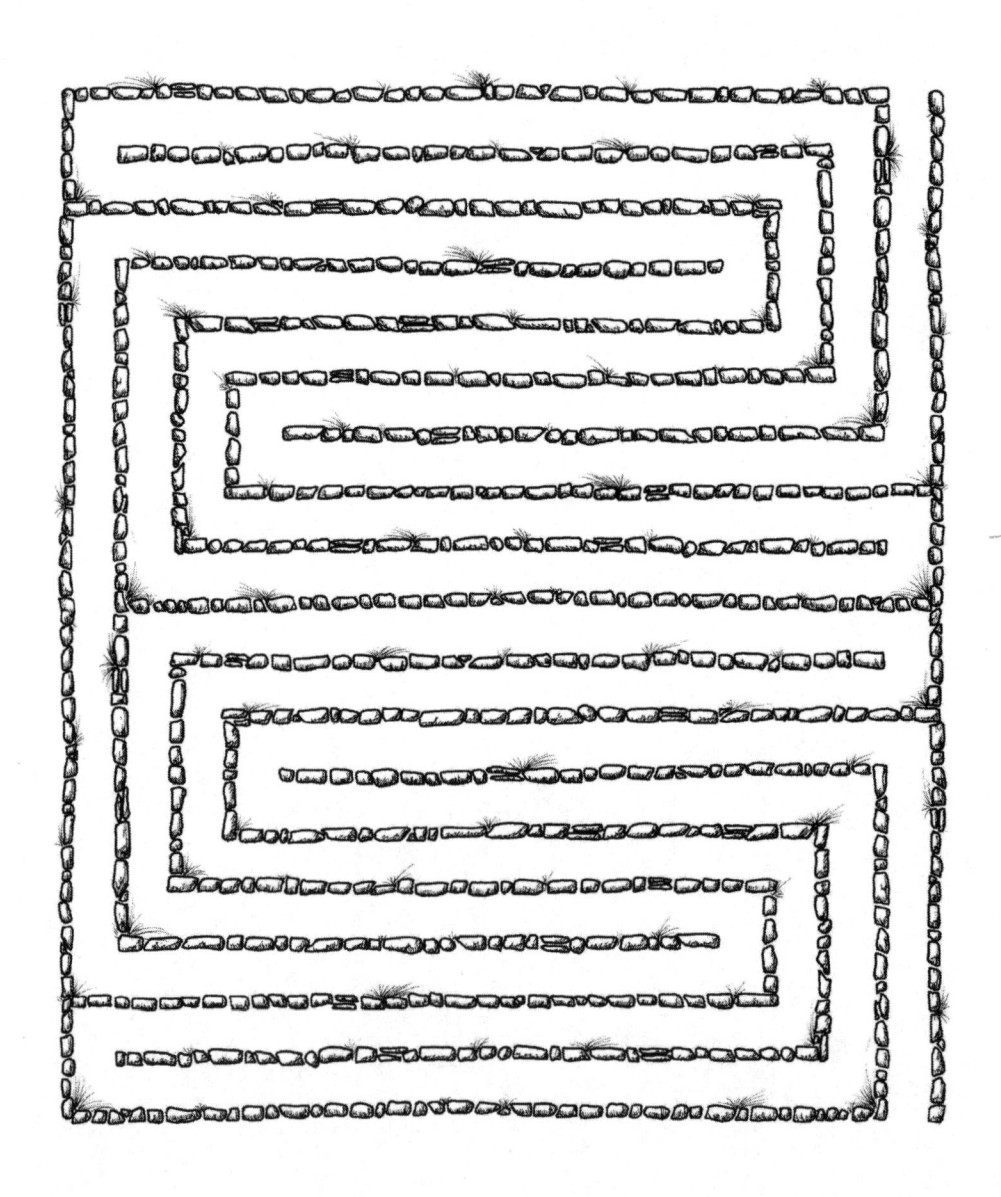

READING

The Lord is my shepherd; I shall not want.
… Surely goodness and mercy shall follow me all the days of my life:
and I will dwell in the house of the Lord for ever.

(Psalm 23:1, 6 KJV)

THINKING

Psalm 23. The Lord is my shepherd and all that. Probably the most well-known bit of the Bible. It's a favourite at weddings and funerals, and it's even the theme tune for *The Vicar of Dibley*.

These song lyrics were written by King David, who was a shepherd before he was famous, so he knew what he was talking about. I can imagine David reminiscing about his childhood on the hills above Bethlehem: how he'd stayed with his sheep through the good times and the bad, by the still waters and through the valley of shadows, how he'd protected them with rod and staff, guiding them along right paths to green pasture. Left to their own devices, his silly and wayward sheep would have got into all sorts of trouble, probably ending up wedged in some rock crevice or stuck halfway down a cliff.

Not that we humans are ever silly or wayward, or ever get ourselves into scrapes and need rescuing. As if!

Then the picture changes from a hillside to a home. The sheep morph into people and the shepherd becomes a homeowner. David is being welcomed in. God prepares a table for him, fills his cup and anoints his head with oil – the ancient equivalent of giving him a nice cup of tea and a choccy biccy.

But this isn't a formal visit, like when you go to see

Great Aunt Maureen and you have to sit politely so as not to mess up the cushions. No, this is coming home after a long time away. This is taking your shoes off and knowing you are safe. This is sinking into the cushions and simply belonging. David closes his eyes and breathes deeply, then takes up his pen and writes: Surely goodness and mercy shall follow me all the days of my life: and I will dwell in the house of the Lord for ever.

I want a bit of that.

RESPONDING

> Gentle Shepherd
> I love this vision of dwelling in your house forever.
> It stirs a distant yearning in me for something I can't find in this life.
> Perhaps it's an echo of Eden, perhaps a future memory of eternity with you.
> But right now, right here, I want a bit of that.
> I want to know the security of home with you.
> Amen.

EXPLORING FURTHER

David wrote a lot of psalms and his greatest hits include Psalms 16, 27 and 32. We'll look at some in the 'Wonder' section, but why not browse a few now?

WALKING

Walk around this stone-built labyrinth and enjoy the solidity and security of its walls. As you walk, imagine you are walking around God's home, and he has invited you to stay. For ever.

PICNIC ON THE BEACH

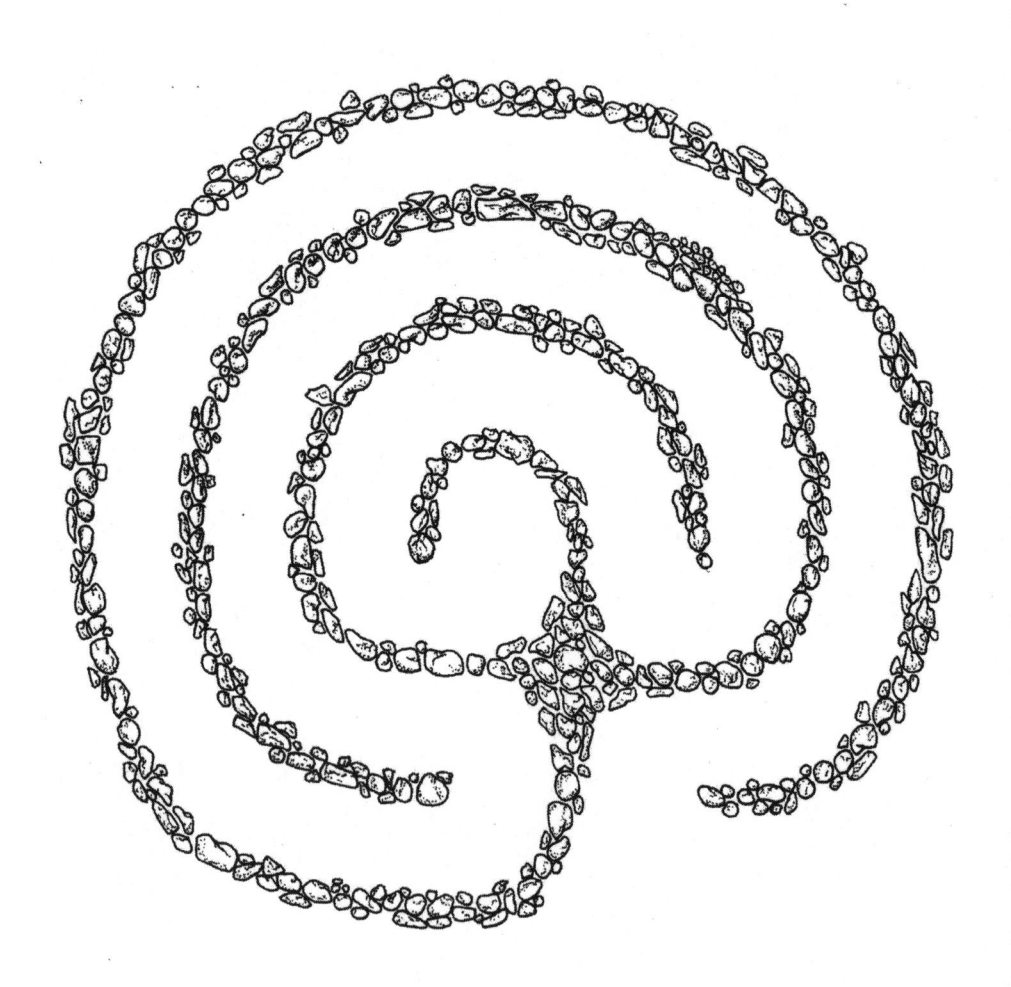

READING

When the followers stepped out of the boat and onto the shore, they saw a fire of hot coals. There were fish on the fire, and there was bread. Then Jesus said, 'Bring some of the fish you just caught.'

When they finished eating, Jesus said to Simon Peter, 'Simon son of John, do you love me more than these?' He answered, 'Yes, Lord, you know that I love you.' Jesus said, 'Feed my lambs.'

Again Jesus said, 'Simon son of John, do you love me?' He answered, 'Yes, Lord, you know that I love you.' Jesus said, 'Take care of my sheep.'

A third time he said, 'Simon son of John, do you love me?' Peter was hurt because Jesus asked him the third time, 'Do you love me?' Peter said, 'Lord, you know everything; you know that I love you!' He said to him, 'Feed my sheep.'

(John 21:9-10, 15-17 NCV)

THINKING

Tables are funny things: some divide – think of the job interview, or the headmaster's study, where the desk makes it clear who's in charge. But other tables welcome and invite, they draw people in saying, 'Come, join us. There's a place for you right here.' A chair is pulled out and you slip into the gap, eating and drinking with your new family. This was the table of the Last Supper, where Jesus dined with his friends before his death. It was also the table – OK, picnic mat – where he ate with them a few days later on the shore of the lake, and where the risen Jesus reinstated Peter.

Peter, who had failed Jesus so badly when he was arrested. Peter, who had abandoned his best friend when he needed him most. Peter, who, when the going got tough, got going in the opposite direction. Three denials. 'I don't bloody know the guy!' Three assurances. 'You know that I love you.' And those assurances weren't for Jesus' benefit – Jesus already knew Peter's heart – they were for Peter to know himself.

I'm sure the grilled fish tasted so much sweeter once that load was off his chest. (A reminder to me to keep short accounts with God.)

But I wonder, is God still in the habit of meals? There is a famous picture by Rublev sometimes called 'The Three Visitors'. It depicts God as three people around a table, from the story in Genesis 18. The artist has placed them on only three sides of the table with the side facing the viewer left open. There is a place for me at the table. I wonder if I will accept the invitation.

RESPONDING

Father God,
You invite me to sit with you and eat,
you draw me into the warmth,
you welcome me into your family.
It's good to be home.
Thank you.
Amen.

EXPLORING FURTHER

It's worth reading the whole of this lovely chapter. Put yourself in the story. Who would you be? What would you say or do?

WALKING

I can imagine Peter skulking on the beach, kicking a few pebbles, as he wonders how he is going to face Jesus. Then he is invited to sit and eat. He is forgiven. Restored. What a relief! As you walk on the sand between the pebbles of this labyrinth, unburden your heart, seek forgiveness and hear God's words of restoration.

AT MARTHA AND MARY'S

READING

As they continued their travel, Jesus entered a village. A woman by the name of Martha welcomed him and made him feel quite at home. She had a sister, Mary, who sat before the Master, hanging on every word he said. But Martha was pulled away by all she had to do in the kitchen. Later, she stepped in, interrupting them. 'Master, don't you care that my sister has abandoned the kitchen to me? Tell her to lend me a hand.'

The Master said, 'Martha, dear Martha, you're fussing far too much and getting yourself worked up over nothing. One thing only is essential, and Mary has chosen it—it's the main course, and won't be taken from her.'

(Luke 10:38-42 MSG)

THINKING

I'm a Martha. I like to be busy. Friends nag me for doing other things while I'm watching a film. 'Can't you just relax and enjoy it?' But … but … if I just sit and watch, my hands will get fidgety, and my mind will get stressy about wasting time goggling at a screen. And then I feel guilty for feeling that way. I should want to 'waste' time with my loved ones, shouldn't I?

I do sympathise with Martha. She wanted to sit with Jesus, like Mary was doing, but someone had to get things ready. The sandwiches weren't going to make themselves. If Mary helped, they'd be finished quicker and then they could both listen. Martha's complaint wasn't unreasonable.

Jesus answered enigmatically. He didn't tell Mary to help, but he didn't tell Martha to sit either. He spoke gently and soothed

Martha's frazzled soul. There were more important things than sandwiches.

We don't know what happened next. We don't know if Martha went back to the kitchen grumbling, or if she stopped and sat by her sister. Had it been me, I'd have brought the bread and butter in and listened while I spread.

Martha and Mary were different, and that's OK.

It's good to 'waste' time with those we love, be that family, friends, or God. But we don't need to feel guilty if we concentrate better when our hands are active. It's OK to be a Martha. She was showing her love with her actions. And we don't need to feel guilty if we're not the three-jobs-at-the-same-time type. It's OK to be a Mary. She was showing her love with her time.

Jesus' point was that you don't *have* to be always doing, doing, doing. 'Being' is good too. Our culture values busyness and we can miss the joy of simply sitting at Jesus' feet. That's why I like labyrinths. They help me to catch a bit of Mary time. And that is good.

RESPONDING

Lord Jesus,
When I'm a bit too Mary,
remind me that my faith
needs expression in real life.
And when I'm a bit too Martha,
call me to come, sit at your feet
and just be.
Amen.

EXPLORING FURTHER

Martha and Mary, together with their brother Lazarus, were some of Jesus' closest friends. You can read more about them in John 11.

WALKING

This Celtic knot design is two intertwined paths, like two labyrinths that weave through each other. Just as we need both halves to make the complete design, so we need both the active Martha and the contemplative Mary in our faith lives. Start at a corner and colour one path as Mary, relaxing into time spent with God, then colour the other path as Martha, asking how your faith might find a practical out-working today.

STAYING FOR TEA

READING

Jesus was going through the city of Jericho. A man was there named Zacchaeus, who was a very important tax collector, and he was wealthy. He wanted to see who Jesus was, but he was not able because he was too short to see above the crowd. He ran ahead to a place where Jesus would come, and he climbed a sycamore tree so he could see him. When Jesus came to that place, he looked up and said to him, 'Zacchaeus, hurry and come down! I must stay at your house today.'

Zacchaeus came down quickly and welcomed him gladly. All the people saw this and began to complain, 'Jesus is staying with a sinner!'

But Zacchaeus stood and said to the Lord, 'I will give half of my possessions to the poor. And if I have cheated anyone, I will pay back four times more.'

Jesus said to him, 'Salvation has come to this house today, because this man also belongs to the family of Abraham. The Son of Man came to find lost people and save them.'

(Luke 19:1-10 NCV)

THINKING

Heaven is going to be a funny old place. I wonder who will be there. Mother Teresa of course, and Martin Luther King. Vicars and curates and nuns, I suppose. All the people at church (except Mr Scroggins who plays the organ out of tune). But there's that guy I read about who was a gang member and drug dealer but then found God in prison. Will I have to share heaven with him, making polite conversation and pretending I don't know what he's done?

I sincerely hope not!

Let me be clear. I don't mean that I hope he won't be there. I mean that I hope that heaven is a darned sight better than polite chit-chat and keeping up appearances. None of us will be in heaven because we've earned our place. Neither me nor Mother Teresa nor cheating, thieving Zacchaeus. (What? You thought he was rich because chief tax collectors earned a high salary?) '*If* I've cheated anyone,' says Zacchaeus. *If?* You know you have, son.

But before I look down my nose at him (easy because I'm 5' 10' and he's a short-arse) I need to remember that we're no different, him and me. We're both in need of God's mercy. We're both of us dressed in filthy rags (that's the Bible's image for our wrong-doings) and both of us are given freshly-laundered clean robes. Phew! What a relief!

Heaven isn't going to be populated with perfect people. It'll be full of people whom God loves. Which includes all kinds of undeserving oiks. Even Zacchaeus. Even that guy from the prison. And even Mr Scroggins on the organ.

RESPONDING

Lord Jesus,
Help me, please, to understand that my worth
is not based on what I do, or have done,
but on your loving-kindness alone.
And that is enough.
Amen.

EXPLORING FURTHER

There's a touching account of Jesus talking with one of the criminals who was crucified next to him, assuring him of his place in paradise. You can read it in Luke 23:32-43.

WALKING

The path through this tree labyrinth has a lot of ups and downs. Sometimes the path is broad, sometimes a narrow squeeze. I'm sure life was a bit like that for Zacchaeus after his grand promises of reform, some parts easier, some parts harder. What is God working on in your life, and how might that be easy or hard at times?

WHO IS JESUS?

It's got to be one of the biggest questions of all time. Who exactly is/was this Jesus?

There's no doubt that Jesus existed. Even Roman and Jewish writers of the time admit that. But was he just another mistaken messiah, or was he really all that his disciples came to believe?

That's not something I can answer for you. But I hope that this small selection of passages, mostly from John's gospel, can help you to think through your answer to the question, 'Who do you say that I am?'

MOVED INTO THE NEIGHBOURHOOD

READING

The Word became flesh and made his dwelling among us. We have seen his glory, the glory of the one and only Son, who came from the Father, full of grace and truth.

(John 1:14 NIV)

THINKING

Imagine the scene: You've just arrived at your favourite summer music festival, wellies and sleeping bag at the ready. You and a bunch of friends are busy with the tents when a guy strolls past with a guitar on his back. 'Mind if I pitch my tent with you lot?' he asks, swinging a holdall onto the grass.

'Sure,' you reply.

He's an ordinary-looking bloke with messy red hair and thick glasses. He disappears later, before the main concert, and doesn't come back until after. You invite him to join you at the campfire and he pulls out his guitar. He's quite good, actually. Turns out his name is Ed.

Sheeran.

It's the same kind of thing when Jesus came to live with us, here. The word that gets translated as 'made his dwelling', really means 'pitched his tent'. When God became human, he came and pitched his tent among us. That has a load of lovely images all rolled up into one.

For starters, it's the headline act living with the fans instead of swanning off to some fancy hotel. God happy to be with us, not snooty and distant.

Next, it's mucky and messy. This isn't a God who's afraid to get his clothes dirty. Bible-time clothes and Bible-time feet would have been covered in dust and sand. Where I live, we have more of a problem with mud, but you get the idea.

And for John's first readers, 'tent' was a powerful reminder of God's presence. In Jesus' time, they had a temple in Jerusalem which was the visible symbol of where heaven met earth. Before that, when the people of God lived in tents in the desert, so did God. There was a special tent which travelled with the people and showed that God was with them.

These days, we don't have a temple or a tent. We have Jesus. Jesus is the symbol of heaven on earth, the place where we can meet with God and know him as we are known.

And I bet he's pretty good on the guitar, too.

RESPONDING

> Lord Jesus,
> thank you for moving into our neighbourhood
> and showing us God's heaven on earth.
> Thank you for becoming like us
> So that we can become like you.
> Thank you for being human who can know us
> and God who can save us.
> Amen.

EXPLORING FURTHER

The start of John's gospel has a beautiful poem that reflects the story of creation in Genesis. Light a candle and imagine that all is dark except that light, and slowly read John 1:1–14.

WALKING

This unusual triple spiral labyrinth has three centres that you visit in turn. It can symbolise the Christian concept of God as three-in-one: creating Father, saving Son, indwelling Spirit. Pray to each character of God as you walk through the paths.

WHO DO YOU THINK YOU ARE?

READING

At this they exclaimed, 'Now we know that you are demon-possessed! Abraham died and so did the prophets, yet you say that whoever obeys your word will never taste death. Are you greater than our father Abraham? He died, and so did the prophets. Who do you think you are?'

'Very truly I tell you,' Jesus answered, 'before Abraham was born, I am!' At this, they picked up stones to stone him, but Jesus hid himself, slipping away from the temple grounds.

(John 8:52-55, 58-59 NIV)

THINKING

'Who do you think you are?'

Jesus faced that question many times. At the start of his ministry, he was challenged in the desert. 'Call yourself the son of God? Yeah, right. Prove it!' In his final hours on the cross, the thief next to him took up the call. 'If you're the son of God, get yourself off this cross. Me too while you're at it.'

And now we see an angry crowd repeating it. 'You're just a jumped-up little nobody. Who do you think you are?'

Jesus' reply sounds odd to our ears. 'Before Abraham ... I am!'

Eh? For a start, that's rubbish grammar, but that's not why the crowd got so angry. I'm sure Jesus had said 'I am' lots of times before. 'Are you hungry, Jesus?' 'I am.' 'Great, let's get pizza.' But this time was different. This was I AM in capitals.

Jesus was quoting from the Old Testament. He did this a *lot,* and his hearers would have understood the reference. We modern readers often don't notice quotations because of differences in culture, time and language, and this can mean we miss the point. So what was Jesus getting at with his D-minus (see me after class) grammar?

Way back in Exodus, Moses had asked God, 'Who are you?' and God had replied, 'I AM.' In capitals.

Oh, yes. Jesus had just called himself by God's name. And the mob knew what he was saying. No wonder they tried to stone him.

Jesus knew who he was. But do you? How would I answer the question? Who do I think I am?

To be honest, that's the wrong question. My opinion of myself does not define me. Nor does the world's. My job title and car don't define me. My education and social status don't define me. My talents and skills don't define me. What matters is who God thinks I am.

Am I his beloved child?

I am.

RESPONDING

Lord God,
It's hard to know who I'm supposed to be,
or who I want to be,
or should be,
or am.
But you call me into your family,
to love as you love me.
And because you are,
I am.
Amen.

EXPLORING FURTHER

You can read about Moses and the strange burning-not-burning bush in Exodus 3. To give you some context, Moses was born to an Israelite slave woman but adopted by an Egyptian princess and raised in the royal household. But when he killed a slave driver, Moses fled for his life and became a sheep farmer in a nearby country. And one day, when strolling through the hills …

WALKING

What would you have made of Jesus' use of God's name? Would you have picked up stones to stone him, or would you have accepted his claim? Step into the central square of this labyrinth, then ponder these questions as you follow the border around to the outside again: who do you think Jesus is, and who does Jesus think you are?

WHAT ABOUT YOU?

READING

Once when Jesus was praying in private and his disciples were with him, he asked them, 'Who do the crowds say I am?'

They replied, 'Some say John the Baptist; others say Elijah; and still others, that one of the prophets of long ago has come back to life.'

'But what about you?' he asked. 'Who do you say I am?'

Peter answered, 'God's Messiah.'

(Luke 9:18-20 NIV)

THINKING

I like Peter. He's great. He's big and loud and he says what he thinks. I could see him today in jeans and a tatty sweatshirt, streak of oil across his forehead and mug of builder's tea in his hand. There's no messing about with Peter. What you see is what you get.

In our reading, we find Peter and the other disciples chatting. They're carefully *not* talking about the Big Question of the day: who is this Jesus guy? They've travelled with him, they've heard what he's said, they've seen what he's done, and they're all thinking the same thing: Could he be The One?

Could this Jesus, this carpenter's son from the first-century equivalent of Tyneside, be God's promised Messiah? ('Messiah' is a Hebrew word meaning 'chosen one'. It's the same as 'Christ'.)

The thought crosses each disciple's mind, and each shakes their head. Nah, don't be daft. He's just a guy. He lives up the road from me. I went to school with his brother. He came round and fixed my neighbour's gate last year.

But then …

He's not just a good teacher. Good teachers don't go around forgiving sins. That's God's job. Good teachers don't say things like, 'Before Abraham was born, I am!' That's God talk. I don't know what to make of him. It'd be easy if he were only the latest fashionable rabbi – listen to the pretty parables, nod your head and say, 'Hmmn, wise,' but that's not the deal here. This is more than nice philosophy. It's a life-changer.

Yeah, and what about being born in Bethlehem, son of David, opening the eyes of the blind, making the lame walk – all the stuff that the Old Testament says the Messiah will do? It sure sounds like Jesus. Couldn't all be a huge coincidence, could it?

Everyone looks at each other. The same thought weighs on each mind, but no one wants to say it. No one wants to risk being the idiot.

So when Jesus broaches the question, they skirt around with various answers, no one admitting what they really think.

Until Peter.

'You are God's Messiah.'

I like Peter.

RESPONDING

Lord Jesus,
I don't have everything straight in my mind.
I don't always know what I should believe
or what I want to believe,
or what I do believe.
But this I do know:
You are good, and kind, and you love me
(though God knows why sometimes)
Is that enough?
    Amen.

EXPLORING FURTHER

If you are wondering who Jesus is, you're not alone. The gospels record a lot of these discussions, and you can read one in John 10.

WALKING

It's OK to have questions. In fact, it's good to have questions; it shows you are engaging with important issues. As you meander through this labyrinth bring your questions to God. It's OK if you don't get immediate answers, because some things are too big for simple one-liners. The important thing is to be honest.

PEACE I LEAVE WITH YOU

READING

Peace I leave with you; my peace I give to you. I do not give to you as the world gives. Do not let your hearts be troubled, and do not let them be afraid.

(John 14:27 NRSVA)

THINKING

What do you want to leave when you're gone?

I don't mean money, something more lasting than that.

Good memories, perhaps? I hope people remember me with fondness. Some people leave park benches overlooking their favourite view. If I die loaded, I might bequeath a library or hospital wing or a university scholarship. Probably not going to happen. More likely it'll be Grandma's ring to my eldest, a donation to cancer research and lots of cakes at my funeral.

Jesus was thinking about this as he sat around the table with his friends. This was his last day of freedom before his impending trial and execution. What could he leave behind for those who had followed him? What would they need in the new world coming?

Peace.

Strong, resilient, rock-solid peace.

Not merely a lack of noise or an absence of war. More than inner contentment; something much more durable. Something they could build a new life, a new faith on.

The Hebrew word for peace, 'Shalom', has a root meaning of wholeness, completeness. In the Old Testament equivalent of accidentally killing the school hamster in the holidays, if you borrowed someone's cow and it died, you replaced the cow to 'shalom' the situation: you restored it, made it whole again. Shalom is completeness, well-being of body, mind and spirit.

That's the Peace that Jesus left.

I love it that Peace was both the last thing Jesus left for his nervous disciples, and the first thing after his resurrection: 'Peace be to you' (see Luke 24:36). Jesus probably said something like, '*Shalom lakhem*', a common Jewish greeting even today.

So what of us? When I look at my life, I know that are plenty of places that need restoring. There are broken bits that need making whole, rough patches that want smoothing, empty gaps that ache to be filled. There's plenty of shalom needed. Fortunately, Jesus has plenty to go around.

'My peace I give you.'

RESPONDING

> God of all comfort,
> Prince of all Peace,
> Holy Spirit who stands alongside me,
> it's easy to fake an outer shell of contentment,
> to pretend that everything is fine
> when it isn't.
> Please breathe your peace into me
> and allow it to flood my being, my mind, my soul.
> Amen.

EXPLORING FURTHER

John 14 is part of a long conversation Jesus had with his disciples before he was arrested. It's full of poignant pictures and memorable sayings. What parts resonate with you?

WALKING

This flower-shaped design leads you around the edge first, then moves deeper in. In the same way, peace may seem a superficial thing at first, a top-coating of stiff upper lip masking the pain. But true peace reaches deep inside, becoming the bedrock upon which all else is built. How far does God's peace reach inside you?

WHO ARE YOU LOOKING FOR?

READING

Jesus spoke to her, 'Woman, why do you weep? Who are you looking for?'

She, thinking that he was the gardener, said, 'Sir, if you took him, tell me where you put him so I can care for him.'

Jesus said, 'Mary.'

Turning to face him, she said in Hebrew, 'Rabboni!' meaning 'Teacher!'

(John 20:15-16 MSG)

THINKING

This is an important question. Who was Mary looking for?

It was early on Easter Sunday morning, and Mary had come to tend Jesus' body. She had known him for several years. She had heard his teaching, witnessed his miracles and seen him forgive sin. Then, only two days ago, she had watched in horror as he was arrested by the Roman forces, tried, condemned, executed and buried. Only two days? More like a million years.

But the body is not in the cave where they left it. Mary is bewildered. Has someone moved it? She glimpses a man nearby and in the dawn half-light, does not recognise him at first.

'Who are you looking for?' he asks.

Good question.

The respectful name she uses means teacher, but was that all he was? If Jesus were only a good teacher, how could he forgive people as if he, a mere human, were the one sinned against? That is God's prerogative alone.

If not a good teacher, then what – God? Or perhaps not

God, but he thought he was. Or not God and he knew it. Those are the only options.

If Jesus knew he was lying when he forgave people, then he was the nastiest conman who ever took breath. If he was sincerely mistaken, then he was a fool who died a meaningless death. The only other option is that Jesus is God, able to forgive the unforgivable, defeating death by dying and living to bring life to all. C. S. Lewis put it like this:

> A man who was merely a man and said the sort of things Jesus said would not be a great moral teacher. He would either be a lunatic – on the level with the man who says he is a poached egg – or else he would be the Devil of Hell. You must make your choice. … You can shut him up for a fool, you can spit at him and kill him as a demon or you can fall at his feet and call him Lord and God, but let us not come with any patronizing nonsense about his being a great human teacher. He has not left that open to us. He did not intend to

In the gathering light of that first Easter, it dawned on Mary who she was looking for.

RESPONDING

> Jesus,
> friend of sinners, forgiver of sin,
> creator, restorer, beginning and end,
> light of the world, way, truth, life –
> help me to see who you are
> and find who I'm looking for.
> Amen.

EXPLORING FURTHER

John's account of the first Easter is probably my favourite. Mary goes to the tomb early, finds it open and tells Peter that the body is missing. Peter and another disciple, perhaps John himself, race to the tomb and peer in. They have no idea what's going on. Then this beautiful meeting between Jesus and Mary and the chapter finishes with Jesus meeting the wonderful tell-it-like-it-is Thomas. All of that in John 20 – fab!

WALKING

Take a morning walk through this garden with Mary, and ask yourself who you are looking for. Will you recognise Jesus when you meet him in the centre?

WATER

Of all the nutrients our bodies need, water is the most important. If need be, we can live for weeks without food, but only three days without water.

The people who wrote and who first read the Bible lived in dry and dusty lands, so water to them was a powerful symbol of refreshing and cleansing, of life and fruitfulness. Those of us who live in rainy places might take water for granted, but for Jesus and his followers, water was Life!

In this section, we'll explore five watery passages, including one from a pop song.

GOD-OFF

READING

Then Elijah stood in front of them and said, 'How much longer will you waver, hobbling between two opinions? If the Lord is God, follow him! But if Baal is God, then follow him!' But the people were completely silent.

(1 Kings 18:21 NLT)

THINKING

Who doesn't love a hot competition, whether it's the World Heavyweight Championship or The Great British Bake Off? They draw huge audiences, and it was the same in Israel, 3000 years ago. In the red corner, Elijah, God's man in an ungodly land. In the blue corner, fighting for rival god Baal, King Ahab and his notorious wife, Jezebel.

Eyes lock. Jaws tighten. Brows lower. You can almost hear the testosterone boiling over. Time for a God-Off.

Ahab told his priests to set up a sacrifice. Elijah got out his deck chair and mocked while they pleaded with Baal to set fire to it. 'Shout louder,' he called. 'Perhaps your god is asleep, or on holiday. Maybe he's on the toilet.'

Funny.

Tactless, but funny.

Elijah's turn. He arranges the sacrifice and, *in the middle of a drought*, drenches it in water! Elijah asks God nicely and POOF! it goes up in a fireball. The crowd rapidly makes up its minds about who's real and who's not.

Wouldn't life be simpler if God did something like that today? Some dramatic sign so that we'd know and believe. Yes, but I don't think it works like that. People don't come to know

God through trumpet-playing angels parading across the sky. (Which is just as well because they'd play merry hell with air traffic control.) Asking for miraculous proof is often an excuse to avoid thinking about it because … well, what if it turns out he's real?

For the Israelites in Elijah's day, it took a spectacular God-Off to shake them out of indecision. Many of us today ignore God until some momentous event brings life's Big Questions forcibly to mind. But perhaps it might be better to think about what we believe before then? Just a thought.

RESPONDING

> Loving God,
> if I'm honest, I'm not sure what I think about miracles
> and things.
> Are they true, or stories with a point?
> But also, if I'm honest, I know that's not important.
> It's an excuse to avoid the real question:
> Are you just a god, or are you The God?
> My God?
> Amen.

EXPLORING FURTHER

I love this event, with Elijah being rude to the other team and then the world's fastest-lighting barbeque. You can read the whole story in 1 Kings 18 starting at verse 17. As for what happened to Elijah next, we thought about that in 'Elijah and The Angel'.

WALKING

The people in Elijah's day had a big decision to make. Was the Lord God real or not? For big questions it is important to consider both sides – don't believe because someone has told you to – it is important to know what you believe. As you walk through first one part and then the other of this double spiral labyrinth, consider the implications if this God-stuff turns out to be a load of hooey, and the implications if it is true.

WEEPING BY THE RIVER

READING

By the rivers in Babylon we sat and cried
  when we remembered Jerusalem.
On the poplar trees nearby
  we hung our harps.
Those who captured us asked us to sing;
  our enemies wanted happy songs.
  They said, 'Sing us a song about Jerusalem!'
But we cannot sing songs about the Lord
  while we are in this foreign country!

(Psalm 137:1-4 NCV)

THINKING

If you're anything like me, you're thinking of the Boney M song when you read this. (If you don't know what that means, ask your parents.) With over two million copies sold, 'By the Rivers of Babylon' has to be the best-selling Bible-disco fusion of all time! Bit of a weird combo, though, isn't it? Why would you put the Bible in a pop song?

I'd swap that question round. Why *wouldn't* you put the Bible in a pop song?

Many of us turn to songs to express our deep-and-meaningfuls, and the people of Bible times were no different. They felt the same fears and sorrows, the same joys and hopes, the same longings and dreams. They put them into songs, which we now call psalms. We've lost the tunes, but the feelings are the same.

This song looked back to a dreadful time for the Jewish people. Their land had been invaded, their temple destroyed, and their people carted off as slaves to Babylon. Now they were sitting by a foreign river, adding their tears to the flow and mourning the life that was gone. And, as if life were not bad enough, their captors were mocking them.

Had God forgotten them, that he let this disaster happen? Did God even know? Did he care? In our own tragedies, we say the same things. We sit by the water and weep for what is lost, for what never will be, and wonder where God is in this.

But here's the good news. God doesn't live in just one country, or in just one time, or in just one place. When the Jewish people were force-marched from their homes, their God walked with them. When we walk through the valley of dark shadow, our Good Shepherd walks with us, rod and staff in hand to beat away the wolves. (That's Psalm 23.)

So it's fine to sit by the waters and weep – some things are worth weeping over – but remember that you don't weep alone.

RESPONDING

>Faithful God,
>Thank you that you walk with me
>when I am far from home,
>and weep with me
>when I am full of sorrow.
>And when I lift my face to you,
>you sing with me by the waters.
>Amen.

EXPLORING FURTHER

Read Psalm 84, about how good it is to be in God's house. The original writer was talking about the Jerusalem Temple, but we can think of the home that God has prepared for us (John 14:2).

WALKING

The people of Israel hung their harps on a tree and wept before God. Walk through this beautiful labyrinth and bring your joys and sorrows to the God who knows and cares.

THE RAIN, IT RAINETH

READING

'You have heard the law that says, 'Love your neighbour' and hate your enemy. But I say, love your enemies! Pray for those who persecute you! In that way, you will be acting as true children of your Father in heaven. For he gives his sunlight to both the evil and the good, and he sends rain on the just and the unjust alike.'

(Matthew 5:43-45 NLT)

THINKING

I live in Britain. It rains. A lot. So here's a very British ditty:

> The rain it raineth on the just
> And also on the unjust fella;
> But chiefly on the just, because
> The unjust hath the just's umbrella.

It's funny but, like a lot of jokes, it hides a nugget of truth, and perhaps a secret fear. If I try to do the right thing, loving my enemy and turning the other cheek, are people going to walk all over me? Will I end up the 'nice guy' who finishes last, soaking wet in a rainstorm because I'm too much of a wimp to do anything about it? It's a reasonable concern. No one wants to be the loser, the butt of everyone's jokes. Is that what Jesus asks of his followers?

No. (Phew!) Jesus isn't telling his followers to be doormats. In his culture, rain was just as much a blessing as sun. God blesses everyone with sunlight, whether they deserve it or not, and God sends rain on everyone's fields, whether they deserve it or not. Rain is a blessing, not a curse (though tell that to Wimbledon).

This unreasonable generosity of God is how his followers are supposed to live, too: loving their enemies and forgiving those who don't deserve it. 'Yes, but, but ...' said Jesus' disciples, 'even if they keep doing it? Even seven times over?'

'Yup,' replied Jesus. 'Even seventy-seven times, or seventy times seven!' (Matthew 18:21-22).

Totally unreasonable. How can anyone be expected to forgive so much? I don't have an easy answer to that. All I can do is remind myself that I'd be grateful for such unreasonable forgiveness if I were on the receiving end. Which I am.

Some people and some actions are harder to forgive than others, but responding with grace instead of an angry knee-jerk is better for my soul and is ultimately healing. I can't control what other people do, but I can control my reaction. I can choose to respond with blessing (through gritted teeth if necessary) instead of curse.

I wonder if dumping a bucket of rainwater on someone's head counts as a blessing?

RESPONDING

Loving God,
I know I should forgive others when they hurt me,
because you forgive me. But it's so hard, sometimes.
I don't want to pray for my enemies.
I want to get back at them!
Lord, when I don't want to forgive,
could you help me *want,* to want to forgive?
Amen.

EXPLORING FURTHER

'Love your enemies' is a famous saying of Jesus, and it's part of a whole collection of pithy teaching called The Sermon on the Mount. We'll visit other parts in other chapters. Here you'll find things like 'blessed are the peacemakers', 'the salt of the earth' and 'turn the other cheek'. It's a high standard to live up to, so you can read Matthew chapters 5 to 7 – if you dare!

WALKING

Follow the swirls of this spinning labyrinth and be drawn into God's loving embrace and unreasonable grace. What do you need to discover at the centre?

WATER FEATURE

READING

Jesus answered, 'Everyone who drinks this water will be thirsty again, but whoever drinks the water I give will never be thirsty. The water I give will become a spring of water gushing up inside that person, giving eternal life.'

The woman said to him, 'Sir, give me this water so I will never be thirsty again and will not have to come back here to get more water.'

(John 4:13-15 NCV)

THINKING

It was lunchtime and the disciples had gone to get food, so Jesus sat down at the well and started chatting to a woman drawing water. To my Western ears, so far, so boring. But in the culture of the time, this was a cartoon-style screech of brakes and an incredulous, 'He did *what*?'

That was the disciples' reaction when they came back with their steaming pasties and take-out coffees. 'What's he doing, talking to her?' 'I dunno. He's always doing weird things.' 'Someone should tell him. It ain't right.' 'Don't look at me.' (Loose paraphrase of verse 27) So what was the problem?

Where do I begin?

For starters, he was talking to a woman, a cultural no-no. Next, she was a Samaritan, a despised nation of half-Jews who had mixed God worship with local idolatry. Any good Israelite would cross the road to avoid meeting one. Oh, and have I mentioned that she was a social outcast? Even among the Samaritans? That's why she was collecting water at the hottest part of the day, not in the morning when the other women went.

But Jesus sat with her anyway and talked to her like she was a human being. He talked about water and she didn't get it at first, thinking he meant the wet stuff in her bucket, but eventually she twigged that he was talking about her.

It reminds me of another conversation that Jesus had, this one with a religious leader called Nicodemus. He was the opposite end of the social scale and supposed to know all this God stuff, but he was slow on the uptake too. Jesus didn't seem to mind though, which is just as well because the disciples do exactly the same thing at the end of this story. Seriously, read the whole chapter. It's hilarious!

The take-home for us is that God's kingdom isn't about knowing all the answers. It's not a test and you don't get a better seat in heaven if you have a theology degree. It's sitting with Jesus by the well in the middle of the day and having a chat about water.

And life.

And stuff.

RESPONDING

Lord Jesus,
I want to be that person who sits and chats with you
and finds out who I am.
I want this living water that you give freely
to all who ask.
I'm asking now.
Amen.

EXPLORING FURTHER

Find out how badly the disciples misunderstood in the rest of chapter 4, or you can read Jesus's conversation with Nicodemus in John 3. We'll meet Nicodemus in 'Pie in the Sky When you Die', but there's no harm in reading it twice.

WALKING

This bubbly labyrinth reminds us of the living water, springing up to eternal life that Jesus talked about. What might that life look like for you?

ANYONE THIRSTY?

READING

On the last day, the climax of the festival, Jesus stood and shouted to the crowds, 'Anyone who is thirsty may come to me! Anyone who believes in me may come and drink! For the Scriptures declare, 'Rivers of living water will flow from his heart."

(John 7:37-38 NLT)

THINKING

It was the final day of Sukkot, the Jewish harvest festival. The crops were safely gathered, and this was party time! At the end of a week's celebration, Jesus gets in another round of drinks then stands on a chair and asks, 'Is anyone thirsty?' Roars of laughter all around and someone accidentally snorts their beer. Jesus liked a joke!

I can see Peter slapping his leg and waving his glass. 'Ha ha! That's a good 'un. 'Anyone thirsty?' Yeah, 'cos we've been drinking sawdust all week. Hey, do you know this one? Three rabbis walk into a bar …'

But Jesus shushes Peter. There's more to say now he has the crowd's attention.

Sukkot celebrations featured pouring water over the altar in the temple. This re-enacted an Old Testament vision of healing water flowing out of the temple, becoming a river that brings refreshment and life to whatever it touches. This same image of God's life-giving water runs through the Bible from Genesis to Revelation.

And Jesus says it's him.

Jesus wasn't asking people if they were thirsty for wine – they'd had plenty – he was asking if they were thirsty for God.

And he was saying that he, Jesus, was the source of refreshment they were looking for.

After all the partying, would they recognise that they were still thirsty?

God is a generous giver, with enough for each and enough for all. There is no condition on the gift of living water. The offer is to anyone, no matter what their past or circumstances or beliefs or fears. All that is needed is to come, and to drink. And then that person will be so full of God's life-giving water that it will overflow like the prophet Ezekiel's vision of the temple.

I can imagine the crowd falling silent. Drinks still in hand they wonder about that ceremony with the water that they'd seen every year. They'd never really thought about what it meant before. There's an air of quiet thoughtfulness. A guy at the back puts his glass down and looks at the man standing on the chair. 'Believe in him?' he thinks. 'Is that all it takes? Because now you mention it, perhaps I am thirsty. Perhaps I always was.'

RESPONDING

> Lord Jesus,
> there's plenty to celebrate in the here-and-now:
> the love of good friends, kindness, beauty.
> But beyond all this, I thirst for something more,
> something further and deeper and higher,
> something more lasting,
> more real.
> I am thirsty, Jesus, and I come to drink.
> Amen.

EXPLORING FURTHER

You can read about the vision of healing water in Ezekiel 47. Old Testament prophets, like Ezekiel, were not fortune-tellers; they were men and women who were in tune with God and not afraid to say what they thought. More *forth*-telling than foretelling, if you like.

WALKING

Walk one side of this whirlpool labyrinth and consider what you are thirsty for. As you pass through the centre, ask yourself what you would like to be thirsty for. As you complete the second side, ask God to give and to quench your thirst.

WONDER

The Psalms are a wonderful collection of poems and song lyrics that you'll find right in the middle of the Bible. They cover the whole range of human feelings, from joy and celebration to gnawing guilt and sorrow, from anger and dismay to trust and hopeful expectation.

Some were written by King David, including the famous Psalm 23, 'The Lord is my shepherd', while others are personal prayers that express longings common to humans across the centuries.

Here's a small selection. You might like to read others and find what resonates with your heart.

STARDUST

READING

The Lord has mercy on those who respect him,
    as a father has mercy on his children.
He knows how we were made;
    he remembers that we are dust.
Human life is like grass;
    we grow like a flower in the field.
After the wind blows, the flower is gone,
    and there is no sign of where it was.

(Psalm 103:13-16 NCV)

THINKING

Looking around my house, I see that I am made of dust. Or rather, dust is made of me.

All those little floating specks that dance in the sunlight – that's me! Plus dirt I've tramped in from outside, and pet hair, and dryer lint, and carpet fluff. But a lot of it is me. In another hundred years, I'll be nothing but dust, wafting around and annoying the heck out of someone by settling on their computer screen. (If computers have screens then. It'll probably be retinal implants or something.)

David was thinking about the impermanence of human lives when he wrote this psalm. I can imagine him looking out over a summer field of grass and flowers. Lush in the green spring, fruitful and strong in early summer, then scorched dry by wind and sun, and gone by winter. Same as all living things. Same as humans in our fragile, temporary bodies.

How long do we live – 80, 90 years? 100 at a push. Compared to trees, that's nothing. Compared to mountains, our lives are the blink of an eye. Less than a blink. We are creatures of time. And not very much of it.

But we are also creatures of eternity. For dust we are, and to dust we shall return, but this dust is known by God. From before the beginning, God knew every molecule, every atom, every quark and muon that make up your body, and which will remain when your body has returned to the dust from which it came. To quote my favourite astrophysicist Neil deGrasse Tyson, 'The atoms of our bodies are traceable to stars that manufactured them … billions of years ago … We are not figuratively, but literally stardust.'

Stardust, known and loved by God. It's kinda cool being dust.

RESPONDING

Loving Father,
You saw the atoms of my body
    long before I was made.
You will see those same atoms
    when they swirl into the outer reaches of space.
Although my time on earth is short,
    in your eyes I am a creature of eternity.
Thank you that you bid me
    spend eternity with you.
Amen.

EXPLORING FURTHER

If you are in a pensive mood, you might enjoy reading Ecclesiastes 3, with its conclusion that we came from dust and to dust we shall return, so in the meantime, we might as well enjoy God's gifts. Ecclesiastes is said to be written by Solomon (Ecclesiastes 1:1), along with Proverbs and the racy(!) Song of Solomon.

WALKING

Our galaxy is made of billions of stars arranged in a spiral. As you walk this labyrinth, see the dots as both stars and dust, ever swirling, the giant and the tiny, all know, all seen, all created by our God. Walk among the dust. Walk among the stars.

RIDING THE WIND

READING

The Lord wraps himself in light as with a garment;
he stretches out the heavens like a tent
and lays the beams of his upper chambers on their waters.
He makes the clouds his chariot
and rides on the wings of the wind.

(Psalm 104:2-3 NIV)

THINKING

I love it when the Bible writers run out of words for describing God and you hear them flailing around for images that are big enough: It's like he wears clothes made of the sun. It's like he lives in a house that fills the whole sky. It's like he drives a sports car as fast as … as … as a hurricane!

OK, not quite so poetic as 'rides on the wings of the wind', but you get the idea.

We can get our knickers in a twist if we mistake these poetic pictures for reality. There was once an argument that the Earth must be in the centre of the solar system because this psalm also says that God 'fixed the earth on its foundations, never to be moved.' If the Earth can't move, then it can't orbit around the sun, so went the reasoning.

But, of course, this psalm isn't about astronomy; it's about security, feeling safe in the care of a mighty God. And the Earth no more rests on giant concrete footings than Jesus grew leaves out of his head when he said, 'I am the vine.' It's important to recognise figurative language when we read the Bible.

So, if this isn't about God riding around in a chariot made of clouds, what is it about?

James Bond. (Stick with me.)

The chariot was the status tech of the culture. Most people who wanted to go somewhere in Bible times, walked. Even a donkey would have been considered posh. Remember that one time when Jesus rode on a donkey? It was so unusual that it was worth mentioning. So a chariot was like Bond's Aston Martin V12 Vanquish – the one with adaptive camouflage so that it could disappear.

So, for a modern take, how about

The Lord wears a laser light show. The Lord lives above the James Webb Space Telescope. The Lord drives a V12 *Vanish*.

Now that's impressive!

RESPONDING

>Mighty and awesome God,
>I don't have the words to describe you.
>I'd say, 'You are more powerful than a crashing storm,'
>but that doesn't even come close.
>I'd say, 'You are more tender than a mother hen,'
>but that doesn't tell the half of it.
>I'd say, 'You are more … more …'
>More than I can think or say or tell.
>I simply don't have the words.
>Amen.

EXPLORING FURTHER

This psalm is full of word pictures describing God. Have a look through and pick your favourites, or why not try writing a few of your own?

WALKING

This hexagonal labyrinth reminds me of the microscopic grandeur of a snowflake. But a snowflake is so tiny, and there are millions, billions falling each winter. The total amount of unseen beauty is more than my mind can take in. And yet that is only a fraction of God's beauty. As you walk through this labyrinth, think of the most of any good quality that you have seen in life. God is more than that.

ALWAYS WITH ME

READING

You have searched me, Lord, and you know me.
You know when I sit and when I rise;
you perceive my thoughts from afar.
How precious to me are your thoughts, God!
How vast is the sum of them!
Were I to count them,
they would outnumber the grains of sand—
when I awake, I am still with you.

(Psalm 139:1-2, 17-18 NIV)

THINKING

Wilma:	Fred, darling, what are the three little words that melt any woman's heart?
Fred:	Let's go bowling?
Wilma:	Not quite, honey. I mean the words you used to whisper when we were dating.
Fred:	Where's your dad?
Wilma:	No, sweetie. Don't you remember? Starts with 'I'. Three words. Eight letters.
Fred:	Oh yes. *Those* words. The words that mean so much between a husband and wife.
Wilma:	Yes Fred, dearest. Will you say them now, for me?
Fred:	[*holding her hands and gazing deeply into her eyes*] I got food.
Wilma:	You know me so well.

Being known is risky. Allowing someone inside our protective fence makes us vulnerable. It can be immensely rewarding, but it can also be hurtful. What if I let them close and they laugh at me or reject me? What if I take off the mask of respectability and let them see me picking my nose, or with my flabby bits out, or when I'm in a bad mood and being very unlovely? Might they not love me anymore?

Being known is risky. And David knew that when he wrote this psalm.

Sure, he was the golden boy, king of Israel, called 'a man after God's own heart'. But he was no plaster saint. David had done some pretty awful things in his life. He was a murderer, adulterer and liar as well as the man who penned 'The Lord is my shepherd'. But here's the take-home – God knew, and still loved him.

And as David he drifted off to sleep each night, he knew he was deeply known and deeply loved. And when he awoke he was still in God's presence. And God spoke into David's soul those three most precious little words. Eight letters. Starts with 'I' I know you.

RESPONDING

Lord,
I'm not sure how I feel about this,
you knowing everything I do and say
even before I do it or say it.
It feels safer to pull up the drawbridge,
to keep you safely at a distance.
Because, what if you see the real me,
and you don't like me?
But then, to be fully known and fully loved …
maybe that's worth the risk?
Amen.

EXPLORING FURTHER

You can read about one of David's less-than-impressive moments in 2 Samuel 11, and how he said sorry in Psalm 51.

WALKING

Being known is dangerous. Being known is hard. As you slowly traverse this labyrinth, each round a little closer in, imagine that you are allowing God to strip away the protective layers, allowing yourself to be known.

WHAT ARE HUMANS?

READING

When I look at your heavens, the work of your fingers, the moon and the stars that you have established; what are human beings that you are mindful of them, mortals that you care for them?

(Psalm 8:3-4 NRSVA)

THINKING

I once went on holiday to Samos, a Greek island famous for sun, sand and mathematicians. (That's my idea of fun, OK? Everyone's a little quirky.) Samos's most famous son is Pythagoras, him of the squares on the hippopotamus and all that, but another big name (literally!) is Aristarchus. He was the guy who first worked out that the sun is in the middle and the Earth goes around it, and he did that nearly 2000 years before Copernicus.

I'm a big fan of Aristarchus. It takes quite a leap of imagination to see that this world we live in, all that we can see or know, is not the centre of the universe. I mean, you only have to look at the sky: sun, moon – everything appears to revolve around me. It appears to, but it doesn't.

I tend to be quite ego-centric. I place things on a map by how far they are from *me*. People are old or young depending on whether they are older or younger than *me*. (And yes, the police are getting younger every year.) But then I step outside and look at the stars and regain some perspective. The psalm writer, thousands of years before me, did the same. I see the pinpricks of light that might be hundreds, thousands or millions of lightyears away from me. Each dot the centre of another solar system, surrounded by planets and maybe even populated by creatures looking up at their stars and wondering the same as me.

My house is just one of thousands in my town, which is one of thousands in my country, which is off the coast of a smallish continent on a blue-green marble circling an average star in a typical galaxy amongst billions of others. What am I that God should even notice me, let alone care?

And yet he does. He knows my thoughts before they form, he sees my going out and my coming in, and even the hairs on my head are numbered.

It's all quite mind-blowing.

RESPONDING

> God of the vast expanses of space,
> God who knows me,
> God of the far reaches of time,
> God who made his home in my neighbourhood,
> you see me.
> Amid the billions of galaxies,
> the trillions of lives,
> you see me.
> And I am amazed.
> Amen.

EXPLORING FURTHER

Paul wrote to the Christians in Philippi (modern Greece) encouraging them to approach God with confidence in his love and care. 'Do not worry about anything, but pray and ask God for everything you need, always giving thanks. And God's peace, which is so great we cannot understand it, will keep your hearts and minds in Christ Jesus.'

You can read this and more in Philippians 4.

WALKING

It amazes me that we can approach such a mighty God and be greeted not with a stern, 'Who are you? What do you want?' but with a kindly, 'I wondered when you'd get here.' This star labyrinth approaches nearer and nearer, finally arriving at the centre. How would you feel, approaching God?

THE HEAVENS DECLARE

READING

The heavens declare the glory of God;
    the skies proclaim the work of his hands.
Day after day they pour forth speech;
    night after night they reveal knowledge.
They have no speech, they use no words;
    no sound is heard from them.
Yet their voice goes out into all the earth,
    their words to the ends of the world.
In the heavens God has pitched a tent for the sun.
(Psalm 19:1-4 NIV)

THINKING

I'm not much good at poetry. I'm limited to the likes of:

> A woeful young bard from Japan
> whose limericks never would scan
> said, 'Pondering why,
> I think it's 'cos I
> get as many words into the last line as I can.'

Or how about haiku?

> Writing a poem
> with seventeen syllables
> is very diffic ...

Fortunately, the writers of the Bible were much better, and the psalms are full of vivid imagery exploring great ideas: a sky full of stars telling of God's greatness; the wordless message spanning the globe; God pitching a tent for the sun … hang on. A tent? Is the Bible telling me that the sun, a ball of hydrogen undergoing nuclear fusion at millions of degrees, lives in a gazebo? I'm sorry, but I believe in science, and I can't believe that.

Sound familiar? How often do we hear the 'science and faith are opposites' trope from popular media? It's an easy headline with the battlelines ready-drawn. Did God make us or Darwin? Is the earth 4.6 billion years old or 6000?

Don't worry, it's not necessary to have one's brain surgically removed to be a Christian. It is quite possible, even normal, to believe both science and the Bible. Many of our greatest scientists were Christians – Galileo, Faraday (electric motors), Mendel (genetics), Lemaître ('big bang') and Collins (human genome) to mention a handful.

One of my favourite quotes is from Nobel-Prize-winning physicist William Bragg, who said that science and faith are opposed only in the way that our thumbs and fingers are opposed, and between them we can grasp anything. Science and faith ask different questions and we need both.

So it's OK to embrace both science and faith, although the Bible has better poetry than most science textbooks. Perhaps I should redress the balance:

> Roses are red,
> violets might be too,
> if their relative velocity
> affects the perceived hue.

Sigh. I'll leave it to the psalms.

RESPONDING

Lord God,
thank you for creating a world of wonder and beauty,
and thank you for science
which helps us to explore and understand.
Thank you that we can use our brains to worship you
as well as our hearts and imaginations.
Amen.

EXPLORING FURTHER

Read the creation story from Genesis 1, enjoying the message that you are precious to God and made in his image, and remembering that it's poetry, not science. (BTW, in case you are wondering, nowhere does the Bible say that the Earth is 6000 years old. It really doesn't.)

WALKING

We sometimes categorise ideas as either 'right-brained' (creative, emotional and intuitive) or 'left-brained' (logical, rational and fact-based). The truth is that both sides of our brains are used in forming true ideas, and we use both fact and intuition together, both logic and creativity, both emotion and reason. As you traverse the two sides of this labyrinth, think about how you can know God in more creative, imaginative ways, and how through more rational, scientific ways. We need both.

RESTORATION

The one thing that is guaranteed in life (besides death and taxes) is imperfection. No job is perfect, no home is perfect, no person is perfect – no, not even one's significant other – and certainly not me. Should I ever find the perfect church, I'll be careful to stay well away because I'd spoil it if I joined!

Our selfie-fixated culture encourages us to present photoshopped perfection, but we live in the cutting room of failed takes and bloopers, and the mismatch between reality and expectation can be troubling.

So it is refreshing that God gives us an honest assessment. We're all damaged – a few chips here, a crack or two there, a bit of a wonky leg (or am I thinking of my dining table?) But that's OK God is in the restoration business.

I WILL GIVE YOU REST

READING

'Come to me, all who are tired from carrying heavy loads, and I will give you rest. Place my yoke over your shoulders, and learn from me, because I am gentle and humble. Then you will find rest for yourselves because my yoke is easy and my burden is light.'

(Matthew 11:28-30 GW)

THINKING

'Place my yoke over your shoulders,' says Jesus.

'Ummn, no thanks,' I reply. 'A yoke sounds like hard work and I don't want loads of "Thou shalt" this and "Thou shalt not" that.'

'Good,' says Jesus. 'I don't want that either.'

Most of Jesus' audience were agricultural labourers, so they knew about heavy loads and hard work. If you wanted to get that sack of corn to market, you carried it on your back. Even everyday tasks were a slog. You want bread for lunch? Start by grinding the flour. You want to get that stain out of the kid's clothes? (Don't ask what it is, you don't want to know.) Start by making the soap. People would be worn out by the end of the day. They knew about tired.

So why would Jesus invite them to take his yoke?

A yoke had two meanings for Jewish people. The first was what you put on a cow's neck so that it could pull a plough. Or rather – and this is important – you put it on *two* cows' necks. Yokes meant sharing the load, working together, the older guiding and training the younger.

And that's where the second meaning comes from. Jewish

people would take on 'the yoke of the Torah' (Moses's teachings) not as a burden, but as a guide for good living.

The trouble was that by Jesus' time, people were living under much heavier loads than Moses' laws. It wasn't just physical life that was tiring; religious leaders had made faith life tiring too, their hundreds of rules very much the letter of the Law, not the spirit.

Jesus was blunt with those who added these millstones to people's backs. When the hierarchy criticised him for not observing rituals he said, 'They crush people with unbearable religious demands and never lift a finger to ease the burden.' (Matthew 23:4 NLT)

Ouch!

Then Jesus says, 'Come to me, you who are flaked out, fed up, fit to drop, and let me ease your load.'

'My yoke is easy.'

'My burden is light.'

'Come, find rest for your souls.'

And ... breathe.

RESPONDING

Lord Jesus,
you bid me come and find rest,
and that sounds good.
You bid me take your yoke,
and that sounds a little scary,
but you say it is easy and light,
so I suppose I could risk it.
Because I could do with some rest.
Amen.

EXPLORING FURTHER

Isaiah 40 explores God's character, ending with the poignant, 'Those who hope in the Lord will renew their strength. They will soar on wings like eagles; they will run and not grow weary, they will walk and not be faint.' Have a read and see which part speaks to your heart.

WALKING

Take a rest under this tree and, when you are ready, allow Jesus to lead you through. You can pause in the centre for as long as you like. When you come out, notice what has changed.

PIE IN THE SKY WHEN YOU DIE

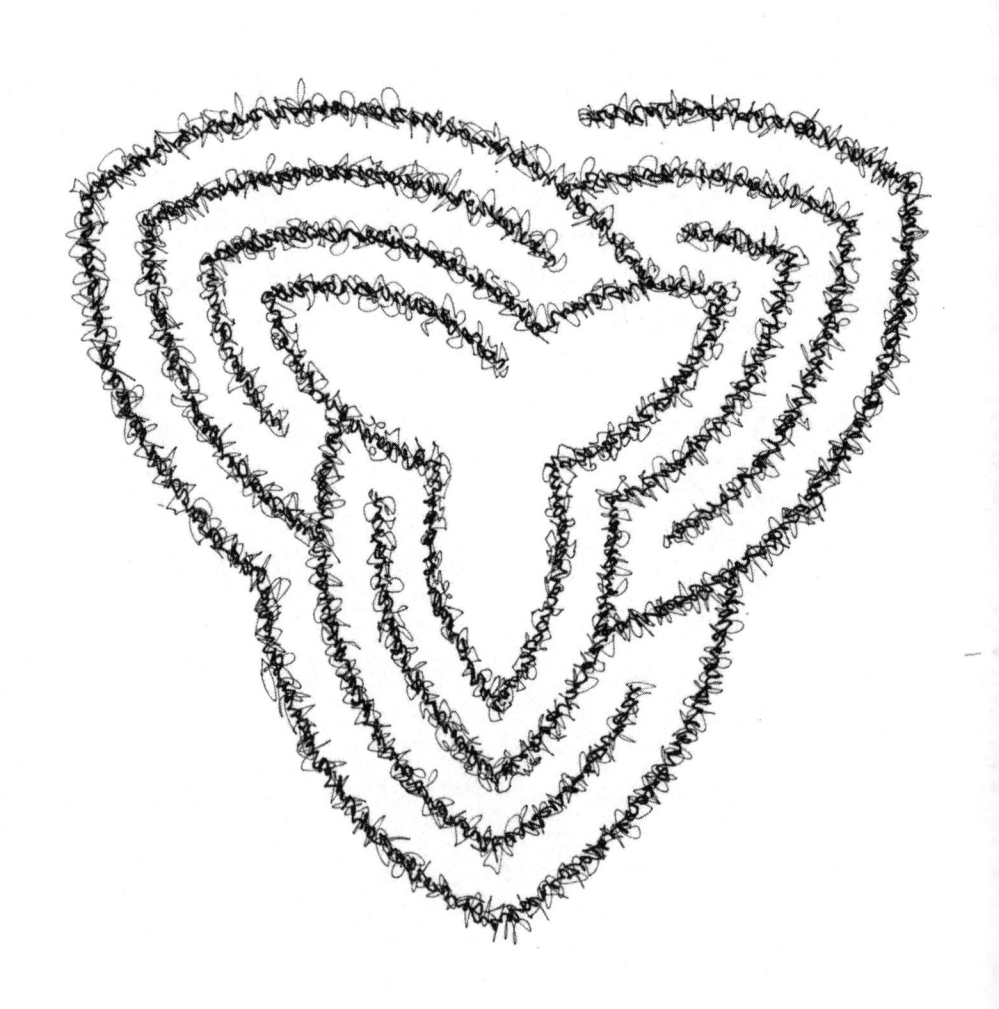

READING

This is how much God loved the world: He gave his Son, his one and only Son. And this is why: so that no one need be destroyed; by believing in him, anyone can have a whole and lasting life. God didn't go to all the trouble of sending his Son merely to point an accusing finger, telling the world how bad it was. He came to help, to put the world right again.

(John 3:16-17 MSG)

THINKING

Eternal life. What does it mean? Going to heaven provided you miss all the fun on earth? That's a popular view of Christianity, but it's pretty much the opposite of what Jesus said.

John 3:16, 'For God so loved the world,' is one of the Bible's famous soundbites. Jesus was replying to Nicodemus, a religious leader who was wondering about life: real life, big life, eternal life. Later in John's gospel, Jesus said he had come to bring life in all its fullness (see John 10:10). Not some watered-down, wishy-washy excuse for an existence, but real-full-bodied Life with a capital L.

This is no empty promise of pie in the sky when you die, this is cake on your plate while you wait! The new life that Jesus promises is not just life *for* eternity, but the life *of* eternity, right here, right now.

God made you, me, each one of us, to know and be known, to love and be loved. When we are separated from God, we feel a yearning that can't be filled with earthly things. We read the story of that separation at the start of the Bible, and the final chapter gives a vision of God and his people reunited forever. But at the moment, we live between the two.

The Bible is a story of restoration, God making ways for humans to be brought near again, and of us humans messing up, time after time. The great Jewish festival of Yom Kippur translates as the Day of Atonement, literally 'at-one-ment', the mending of brokenness, the restoration of that which was. This restoration culminates in Jesus – God come as a human so that humans can come to God. Jesus provides the way for us to know this rich life with God. The life of heaven lived on earth. Life as it was always meant to be.

We live in both time and eternity. We stand with one foot on earth and one in heaven, born of our human parents and, through Jesus, born of God. For God so loved … you.

RESPONDING

Loving God,
Thank you that you came to find me when I was lost.
Thank you that you want me in your family.
Thank you that you offer me Life with you.
I want to be found. I want to be in your family. I want your Life.
Amen.

EXPLORING FURTHER

It's worth reading the whole of Jesus's conversation with Nicodemus in John 3. I love it that this well-educated religious man had no idea what Jesus was talking about at first. Makes me feel not quite so thick. I also love it that we meet Nicodemus again on the first Good Friday, carrying Jesus' body from the cross (John 19). I'm glad he understood eventually.

WALKING

The life of heaven lived on earth. Life restored by Jesus, sent by the Father in the power of the Spirit, to bring life as it was always meant to be. As you walk this labyrinth, moving inwards, outwards, then inwards and finally reaching the centre, consider your journey towards life. For many of us, the journey is not smooth but that does not matter provided you keep moving toward God.

ALL IN THE SAME BOX

READING

But now God has shown us a way to be made right with him without keeping the requirements of the law, as was promised in the writings of Moses and the prophets long ago. We are made right with God by placing our faith in Jesus Christ. And this is true for everyone who believes, no matter who we are.

For everyone has sinned; we all fall short of God's glorious standard. Yet God, in his grace, freely makes us right in his sight. He did this through Christ Jesus when he freed us from the penalty for our sins.

(Romans 3:21-24 NLT)

THINKING

When the first trains ran through the channel tunnel, French tourists arrived at Waterloo, named after Napoleon's defeat I wonder if that was deliberate. It's St Pancras International now, which isn't nearly as funny.

The English and French have long used each other as the butt of gentle humour. English call the French 'Frogs', and they return the insult with 'Rostbif'. Us and Them. Like Star Wars fans and Trekkies.

It was the same in Jesus' time. Us good Jewish folks, and Them: Samaritans and Gentiles. It was clear whom God loved. So when Jesus told his story about the *Good* Samaritan, it was shocking. No such thing! When he sat and talked with a Samaritan woman, his disciples were so gob-smacked they didn't even know how to complain. And what about Gentiles like the occupying Roman army? Did God love them? Not a chance! But Jesus spoke with them, and healed them – talk about fraternising with the enemy!

The Us and Them came to a head when Christianity started spreading. Beginning in Jerusalem, it crossed into surrounding countries and soon expanded throughout the Roman Empire. There was a thriving church in Rome, and it was full of Them. So the hot topic of debate was, 'Does God love Them?'

Yes.

In fact, take any group that is considered Them, and ask 'Does God love Them?'

Yes.

This letter to the Christians in Rome spells it out. Neither Jews nor non-Jews are less loved by God or more in need of mercy. We've all fallen short of the standard and God redeems all of us just the same, no matter who we are.

In Jesus' time, the big question was Jew or Gentile. At various times since it has been White or Black, Man or Woman, Straight or Gay. It won't stop there, I'm sure. Humans seem to like putting people in boxes and sticking on a label that says 'Them'. And God can't love Them.

But the Good News is that God rips off every label, opens every box and says, 'Hello, welcome to my family.' Everyone is Us.

Even the French. I suppose.

RESPONDING

Lord Jesus,
finder of the lost,
teach me, please,
the humility of knowing myself lost without you,
and the joy of knowing myself found.
Amen.

EXPLORING FURTHER

The letter to the Romans is a dense read. It's like rich fruitcake, chock full of wonderful teaching, and best consumed slowly. I recommend chapter 8 especially, which has the whole of Christianity packed into 39 verses.

WALKING

Take a meander through these tumbling blocks and notice the different cubes, the different surfaces, the different directions – turning right going inwards, turning left coming out. The path leads through all. Where might God be nudging you to explore beyond your comfort zone?

FREE GIFT

READING

God saved you through faith as an act of kindness. You had nothing to do with it. Being saved is a gift from God. It's not the result of anything you've done, so no one can brag about it. God has made us what we are. He has created us in Christ Jesus to live lives filled with good works that he has prepared for us to do.

(Ephesians 2:8-10 GW)

THINKING

A few miles down the road from me is the adorably English market town of Olney, famous for stone-built houses, pancake races and the hymn 'Amazing Grace', written by local clergyman, John Newton. Goodness, it's so sweet I'm getting a sugar rush!

But would it sound so chocolate-boxy if I told you that John Newton was a slave-trader?

Yes, the guy who wrote one of the world's favourite hymns was a hard-drinking, hard-swearing trader in human cargo who started his song-writing career with obscene ditties about his captain.

Not so cutesy now, eh?

But Newton reassessed his priorities after nearly drowning in a particularly violent storm, and became a clergyman and abolitionist. When he wrote, 'I once was lost, but now am found/was blind, but now I see,' he really knew what he was talking about.

It's the same story with Paul, the writer of this letter to the Christians in Ephesus, in modern Turkey. Paul wasn't always the kind of guy you'd name a cathedral after. He used to persecute Christians, hunting them down and proudly watching them being stoned. Not a nice guy.

So what happened?

Grace happened.

God's undeserved goodness to a slave-trader, a murderer, a bully, a cheat, a liar … fill in anything you like. God's undeserved goodness to John Newton, to Paul, to me, to you.

OK I've never run a slave ship, and I've never had anyone killed, but that's not the point. There aren't 'little sins' that don't really count and 'big sins' that do. It doesn't matter if I'm 10 metres down a pit or 100 – I still can't get myself out. But as soon as I realise that I need rescuing, a rope ladder appears and God's strong hands haul me up. It's a gift. It's free. It's because I need rescuing and God is nice like that.

Of course, having been rescued, it's expected that I don't chuck myself down the pit again (though if I do, God has plenty of rope ladders). God does not save us *because* of good works, but good works should be the result. Realising we are loved by God should change our lives just as it changed Paul's and John Newton's. Paul realised he was loved and wrote to his friends in Ephesus. John realised and wrote 'Amazing Grace'.

RESPONDING

Amazing Grace (how sweet the sound),
that saved a wretch like me.
I once was lost, but now am found,
was blind, but now I see.
A-bloody-men! (as John Newton might have said).

EXPLORING FURTHER

The whole of Ephesians 2 is about God bringing people into his family and there are some lovely assurances in this chapter. Why not choose your favourite and write it on your mirror?

WALKING

Paul wrote to his friend Timothy saying, 'Here's a word you can take to heart and depend on: Jesus Christ came into the world to save sinners. I'm proof—Public Sinner Number One.' (1 Timothy 1:15 MSG)

Trace your way through this Celtic knot labyrinth and thank God for Jesus who came to save Paul, John Newton, me, and you.

... AS HER GREAT LOVE HAS SHOWN

READING

'Two people owed money to a certain money-lender. One owed him five hundred denarii, and the other fifty. Neither of them had the money to pay him back, so he forgave the debts of both. Now which of them will love him more?'

Simon replied, 'I suppose the one who had the bigger debt forgiven.'

'You have judged correctly,' Jesus said.

Then he turned towards the woman and said to Simon, 'Do you see this woman? I came into your house. You did not give me any water for my feet, but she wet my feet with her tears and wiped them with her hair. You did not give me a kiss, but this woman, from the time I entered, has not stopped kissing my feet. You did not put oil on my head, but she has poured perfume on my feet.

'Therefore, I tell you, her many sins have been forgiven – as her great love has shown. But whoever has been forgiven little loves little.'

Luke 7:41-47 (NIV)

THINKING

I bought my first house for £31,000. You wouldn't get a shoebox for that these days! But it was still way more than I earned in a year. And that's what Jesus was talking about in his story of the two debtors. Five hundred denarii. More than a year's wages. It was a mortgage-sized debt and secured, not on your house, but on you. Now imagine that you have to pay it back. Tomorrow. In cash.

You can't do it. Not a chance. You and your family will be sold into slavery to pay back the bank.

You trudge back home – not your home for much longer – wondering how to break the news to your wife. You've lost everything. You might never see each other again. (Would she even want to? Probably not.)

'And what about the kids?' she'll ask. They'll be sold too, and it's all your fault. They're going to hate you. You hate you.

A text arrives from the bank. The manager wants to see you again. More bad news?

You stand in silence, head down, hands behind your back.

He speaks.

You can't believe your ears. This is just wishful thinking. He can't mean it, can he?

You walk out in a daze.

You look at the pieces of paper in your hands – the halves of a torn-up contract. It must have been real. He forgave your debt right in front of your eyes. Cancelled. No one is getting sold you don't even have to pay the debt back!

You dash into a nearby supermarket on the way home (yes, home!) and buy the best bottle of port you can find and a really nice thank you card. It's not much for such a great forgiveness, but you have to do something.

'Her many sins have been forgiven – as her great love has shown.'

RESPONDING

Loving Lord Jesus,
My debt was piled up like a mountain;
you paid the price and freed me.
I was drowning at the floor of the ocean;
you dived down and pulled me out.
I was far from you and lost;

you found me and brought me home.
'Thank you' seems too small.
But thank you anyway.
Amen.

EXPLORING FURTHER

Jesus taught us to ask forgiveness for our debts (sins, trespasses). You can find this in Matthew 6:9-13 – you may recognise it!

WALKING

This teardrop-shaped labyrinth represents both the woman's tears of grateful love and the perfume that she poured on Jesus' feet. What are you grateful for, and how might you express that gratitude?

FAITH

In Lewis Carroll's *Through the Looking Glass,* the White Queen challenges Alice to believe 'six impossible things before breakfast'. Is that what we mean by faith, screwing up our eyes to convince ourselves of things that we know aren't really true?

Nope. Christian faith has a more solid foundation.

Another Lewis, C. S. this time, the author of the Narnia Chronicles, described faith as an outworking of reason, battling against unstable emotion. 'Faith, in the sense in which I am here using the word, is the art of holding on to things your reason has once accepted, in spite of your changing moods.' Far from faith being the opposite of reason, Lewis regards faith as a result of reason – the faith that keeps me believing in aeroplane wings despite them not looking enough to lift the plane I'm in.

However, faith is only as good as the one in whom that faith is vested. In these five chapters, we will think about who it is that Christians have faith in.

HOW FAR?

READING

He has not treated us as we deserve for our sins
or paid us back for our wrongs.
As high as the heavens are above the earth –
that is how vast his mercy is toward those who fear him.
As far as the east is from the west –
that is how far he has removed our rebellious acts from himself.
(Psalm 103:10-12 GW)

THINKING

Let's get something out of the way. That word 'fear'.

We can get an idea that God is a cross old man sitting on a cloud watching for when we do something wrong and then blasting us with thunderbolts. 'Ha! That'll learn 'em!'

But when the Bible talks about fearing God, it's not fear like being chased by thugs or facing a lion who is licking his lips and reaching for the salt and pepper. Instead, imagine that Steven Spielberg is watching you in a play, or perhaps the King is popping round for tea. Frightened? I'd be like a squid in an ink factory! But not because these people are nasty. I'd be frightened because I want them to think well of me.

Fearing God doesn't mean being frightened, as if God were some monster or bogey-man. It's about respect, awe, worship. Think 'honour' or 'reverence'. So, with that cleared up, if God's not a cross old man on a cloud, what does this psalm tell us that God is like?

God is just. Bad stuff needs dealing with, not brushing under a carpet.

God is kind. He knows that we make mistakes and treats us with mercy and grace.

God is generous. His love for us reaches higher than the heavens.

And most of all, God is a restorer. Like the Japanese art of kintsugi, repairing broken pottery with 'golden joinery', God sees what needs mending and mends it, making our cracks and chips more beautiful in the experience. He picks us up when we fall, washes our bloodied knees and puts us back on the right road. He takes our wrongdoing, screws it up into a ball and drop-kicks it over the horizon, never to be seen again.

Now that sounds like a God worthy of honour. I wonder if he'd like to pop round for tea?

RESPONDING

Loving God,
Thank you that you don't pretend I'm perfect,
   because we both know that I'm not.
Thank you that you treat me with kindness and justice, taking away my wrongdoing through Jesus.
   Thank you that your love for me stretches higher than the heavens
   and right down deep into my soul.
Amen.

EXPLORING FURTHER

Psalm 103 is my favourite psalm (take that Psalm 23!) and we looked at another part of it in the chapter 'Stardust'. Why not have a go at writing an extra verse or two of your own? (Don't worry, no one is going to mark it.)

WALKING

This labyrinth reminds me of a compass rose, pointing North and South, East and West. I love it that God promises to banish our sins as far away as the East is from the West, because that is infinitely far! There is no end or East or West – you can just keep going. As you walk through this labyrinth, use and pencil to write along the path the things that you want God to banish. In the centre, commit them to God and ask forgiveness, then on the way back, rub them out.

BUT SOME DOUBTED

READING

Meanwhile, the eleven disciples were on their way to Galilee, headed for the mountain Jesus had set for their reunion. The moment they saw him they worshipped him. Some, though, held back, not sure about worship, about risking themselves totally.

Jesus, undeterred, went right ahead and gave his charge: 'God authorized and commanded me to commission you: Go out and train everyone you meet, far and near, in this way of life, marking them by baptism in the threefold name: Father, Son, and Holy Spirit. Then instruct them in the practice of all I have commanded you. I'll be with you as you do this, day after day after day, right up to the end of the age.'

(Matthew 28:16-20 MSG)

THINKING

'I told you I was ill.' So reads the headstone of comedian Spike Milligan.

Last words can be important. They live long after the funeral flowers and can serve as a poignant memento of your life. Or not. Among the last words of American Civil War general, John Sedgwick, were, 'They couldn't hit an elephant at this dist ...'.

The end of Matthew's gospel records Jesus's final speech to his disciples. 'I am with you always, to the very end of the age.' Jesus would not leave his friends to cope on their own, but would be with them, wherever and whenever, no longer limited by time or space. And this promise was not just for those first disciples, but for all who follow.

In other words, us.

'Sounds great,' you say, 'but I'm not like those disciples.

They'd seen him. They knew. I'm not so sure. What if all this Christian stuff turns out to be one big misunderstanding?'

Don't fret, my friend. The first disciples were exactly the same. Look a couple of sentences before. Some held back. They weren't sure. These weren't Super-Christians, wearing their knickers over their robes and leaping tall synagogues in a single bound. These were ordinary folks like you and me. Folks with doubts, confusion and uncertainty.

It's OK to not have all the answers. Being a Christian is not about knowing everything (just as well), it's about relationship. And have you noticed what Jesus did about those who doubted?

Nothing.

Jesus treated them all exactly the same. Nobody got told off for having questions. Nobody got a big fat 'F' in faith and had to repeat the year. As Jesus said, even faith as small as a mustard seed is enough if it's faith in a big God.

God knows our confusions and can cope just fine. He sees what we have and says, 'Good, I can work with that.'

Spike Milligan put it well when he said, 'Blessed are the cracked, for they let in the light.'

RESPONDING

Lord Jesus,
Thank you for comforting me
by your promise to be with me always.
Thank you for accepting me
with all my doubts and imperfections.
Thank you for challenging me
to go beyond where I am now.
I'm glad that I don't need to go alone.
Amen.

EXPLORING FURTHER

I know we've looked at John 14 before (see 'Peace I Leave With You'), but it's worth reading again. Jesus is comforting his disciples about his imminent departure and tells them that he will leave them 'another comforter' or 'another advocate' who will be with them always. He is talking about The Holy Spirit, who is God living in the believer. A tricky concept, I know, but Jesus thought it a good idea, so that's fine by me.

WALKING

This labyrinth involves a lot of climbing upwards only to slip back down again. Perhaps you might feel like that in your faith – one step forwards, two steps back. Labyrinths can help us to understand the convoluted nature of life's journey, that steps backwards can be part of the journey forwards. So do not worry. Put your hand in the hand of God, and walk.

LOVE IS ...

READING

Love is patient and kind. Love is not jealous, it does not brag, and it is not proud. Love is not rude, is not selfish, and does not get upset with others. Love does not count up wrongs that have been done. Love takes no pleasure in evil but rejoices over the truth. Love patiently accepts all things. It always trusts, always hopes, and always endures.

Love never ends.

(1 Corinthians 13:4–8a NCV)

THINKING

It's a lovely poem, isn't it? It's popular at weddings, and it looks great on a cutesy plaque hanging in your kitchen. But this is more than an inspirational sound-bite, more than a tea towel to give to your gran. This is a declaration of war!

'War? That doesn't sound very loving,' you object.

Maybe. Maybe not. It depends on what you're fighting against, doesn't it?

This is love that fights injustice, that stands up for the oppressed, that rights wrongs and heals hurts.

This is love with muscles.

We're not talking about some wishy-washy, starry-eyed infatuation. We don't mean sighing over a photo and saying, 'No, *you* put the phone down first.' The kind of love that God is, the kind of love that his children are called to show, is bigger and tougher than twittering doves and glittery hearts.

It's the fierce love of a parent defending their child. It's the love that kneels and trims the toenails of a homeless person. It's the love that speaks out when it's easier to be silent. It's the love that stands alongside the victim and gives them its coat. This is love that fights when it hurts to fight, that forgives when it costs to forgive, that never, ever, *ever* gives up.

Wow. I need a minute to take all that in.

Suddenly, this is not a pretty poem anymore. It's a challenge, a gauntlet thrown down, a bar set *very* high. I feel a total failure when I read this litany of what real love means. I am often impatient and unkind. I get jealous. I brag. I carry resentment. I see faults in others which are really faults in me.

I am so *not* what it says on the tin.

This passage is a manifesto for a different kind of human, and I don't match a fraction of it. But I'm thankful that God matches perfectly.

RESPONDING

> God who is love,
> Thank you that you are patient and kind.
> Thank you that you are not easily angered,
> and keep no record of wrongs.
> Thank you that you never fail.
> Amen.

EXPLORING FURTHER

The same John who wrote the fourth gospel later wrote three letters to help the new Christians understand how to live out their faith. You can read some of his wise advice in 1 John 4 starting at verse 7. (TL;DR – love people.)

WALKING

There are three things that I find interesting about this labyrinth. The first is the wording in the walls. It is taken from 1 Corinthians 13 and reminds me that these words can guide my path, if I will let them. The second is the imperfection. The words are not even, nor are they the same all through, but that is fine. The core is right and the details do not matter so much. The third is the shape. The heart shape at the centre is mimicked on the outside. It is not identical, but the core affects the outer. As it should. What is your core?

LOST AND FOUND

READING

Then Jesus said, 'A man had two sons. The younger son said to his father, "Give me my share of the property." So the father divided the property between his two sons. Then the younger son gathered up all that was his and travelled far away to another country. There he wasted his money in foolish living. After he had spent everything, a time came when there was no food anywhere in the country, and the son was poor and hungry.

'When he realized what he was doing, he thought, "All of my father's servants have plenty of food. But I am here, almost dying with hunger." So the son left and went to his father.

'While the son was still a long way off, his father saw him and felt sorry for his son. So the father ran to him and hugged and kissed him.'

(Luke 15:11-14, 17, 20 NCV)

THINKING

'Once upon a time … they all lived happily ever after.' In fairy tales, baddies get their comeuppance and heroes are home in time for tea. But life is rarely that simple, and it's not always clear who are the heroes and the baddies.

Jesus is talking to a group of 'less socially acceptable' people, as he often did. The religious leaders were complaining about it, as they often did. And Jesus told a story. 'Once upon a time, there was a man who had two sons …'

The younger son demands half his father's money and blows it on wild parties. When the money goes, so do his 'friends', and he's reduced to cleaning public toilets during the day and sleeping there at night. 'You're so stupid!' he yells at himself. 'Go back and work for Dad. At least your bed won't stink of pee and bleach.'

Dad has been watching for him all the time he's been away and spots him far down the road. Arms flung wide and sandals flying off, the dad dashes to meet his son, tears running down both their faces. Happily ever after? You'd think so, wouldn't you?

But the party that follows is not popular with the elder son. The good boy. The one who stayed home and kept his nose clean. He's jealous. This isn't how stories work. The baddie isn't supposed to be welcomed home with a steak roast. The elder brother stands outside and seethes.

Dad notices and goes to find him. 'My son, you are always with me, and everything I have is yours.' This wasn't a zero-sum game, where more love for one son meant less love for the other. Both were wanted.

The listening crowd knew Jesus was talking about them, whether they were the younger son, knowing he needed forgiving, or the older son who hadn't realised he was lost.

We don't know how the story ends, but I hope they managed their version of happily ever after.

RESPONDING

Jesus,
find me please,
because I am lost.
Amen.

EXPLORING FURTHER

Once again, I've had to massively abbreviate this famous tale. You can read the whole story in Luke 15, together with a couple of others on the same theme. Jesus really wanted to get this message across, loud and clear!

WALKING

This is another design based on a Celtic knot. Here I have untwisted two opposite corners so that we have two separate paths. One is for the father in Jesus's story, one for the son. You will see that they start together but then drift apart, hardly even touching. Perhaps there are areas in your life that feel like this. The paths join again at the end. Where is God in this for you?

AARON'S BLESSING

READING

May the Lord bless you and keep you.
May the Lord show you his kindness
   and have mercy on you.
May the Lord watch over you
   and give you peace.

(Numbers 6:24-26 NCV)

THINKING

In younger days, I used to sing these words as a lullaby to my best friends' children. When I had children of my own, I soothed them with the same song. One day I may have grandchildren and sing to them as well.

It's a beautiful prayer, and that's hardly surprising since God wrote it. God told Moses to tell his brother Aaron to pray it over the Israelites, and it is still used in synagogues today. That's the same prayer being prayed for more than 3,000 years! For the history geeks, Moses and Aaron were contemporaries of Rameses II, aka Ozymandias, from that poem you might have done at school.

That's lovely. An ancient prayer that we can admire as history. A lullaby for the kiddies. I even got a poet in there. How very educational. So what? Is the Bible only beautiful poetry from ancient cultures and pretty stories for children? Is Christianity only useful as a comfort for the dying and a crutch for the weak, or is it something more?

Of course I'm going to say it's more, but I'm in good company. Brilliant minds the size of Thomas Aquinas, J. S. Bach and J. R. R. Tolkien's have believed God is real and knows each of us personally. It's not something they can prove evidentially, any more than I can prove that my mum loves me, but I'm pretty sure she does, and I'm pretty sure God does, too.

So what difference does that make in my life, in your life?

It means that we don't have to try to be good so that God will like us. He does already.

It means that faith is not about rules; it's about being known, really known, and loved anyway (although a living faith will change us in ways we cannot tell).

It means that God comes to us in Jesus, and holds out his hand to bring us home.

Bear Grylls puts it well when he says, 'To me, my Christian faith is all about being held, comforted, forgiven, strengthened and loved – yet somehow that message gets lost on most of us, and we tend only to remember the religious nutters or the God of endless school assemblies. This is no one's fault, it is just life. Our job is to stay open and gentle, so we can hear the knocking on the door of our heart when it comes.'

Are you ready to hear?

RESPONDING

> Lord, bless me and keep me.
> Show me your kindness
> and have mercy in me.
> Lord, watch over me
> and give me peace.
> Amen.

EXPLORING FURTHER

Jesus encourages us to approach God confidently. 'Ask, and it will be given you,' he says. 'Seek and you will find. Knock and the door will be opened.' You can read this, and a whole load more in Matthew 7.

WALKING

This simple spiral labyrinth has a path that is easy to see; there is no confusion about the destination or the path. Yet still, the journey is full of change. The ground underfoot varies from sticks to leaves to cobbles. The width changes – some parts are narrower, perhaps hurried, while the broader parts might be full of crowds and slower to traverse. Walk slowly and consider your travels with God. And may he give you peace. Amen.

QUOTATIONS

Introduction: Martin Luther King in Bredenberg, J., ed., 2006, *Treasury of Wit & Wisdom*, p 46.

Whole Food: St Augustine, tr. by Edward Bouverie Pusey, 398 (2009), *The Confessions of Saint Augustine*.

Picnic on the Beach: Andrei Rublev, fifteenth century, *Trinity* or *The Hospitality of Abraham*.

Who are you Looking For?: C. S. Lewis, 1952, *Mere Christianity*, ch 3.

The Rain, it Raineth: Charles Bowen in Brandreth, Gyles, ed., 2013, *Oxford Dictionary of Humorous Quotations*, p 314.

Stardust: Neil deGrasse Tyson, 2010, *Neil deGrasse Tyson answers your questions*, https://www.reddit.com/r/IAmA/comments/bwe6j/neil_degrasse_tyson_answers_your_questions/

The Heavens Declare: William Bragg, 1920, *The World of Sound*, p 196.

Faith: C. S. Lewis, 1952, *Mere Christianity*, ch 12.

Aaron's Blessing: Bear Grylls, 2011, *Mud, Sweat and Tears*, p 93.

BIBLE QUOTATIONS:

ICB – Scriptures quoted from the International Children's Bible®, copyright ©1986, 1988, 1999, 2015 by Tommy Nelson. Used by permission.

KJV – Scripture taken from the King James Version. 1611.

MSG – Scripture quotations marked MSG are taken from THE MESSAGE, copyright © 1993, 2002, 2018 by Eugene H. Peterson. Used by permission of NavPress. All rights reserved. Represented by Tyndale House Publishers, Inc.

NCV – Scripture taken from the New Century Version®. Copyright © 2005 by Thomas Nelson. Used by permission. All rights reserved.

NIV – Holy Bible, New International Version® Anglicized,

NIV® Copyright © 1979, 1984, 2011 by Biblica, Inc.® Used by permission. All rights reserved worldwide.

NLT – Scripture quotations marked NLT are taken from the Holy Bible, New Living Translation, copyright © 1996, 2004, 2015 by Tyndale House Foundation. Used by permission of Tyndale House Publishers, Inc., Carol Stream, Illinois 60188. All rights reserved.

NRSVA – New Revised Standard Version Bible: Anglicised Edition, copyright © 1989, 1995 the Division of Christian Education of the National Council of the Churches of Christ in the United States of America. Used by permission. All rights reserved.

TLB – Scripture quotations marked (TLB) are taken from The Living Bible, copyright © 1971 by Tyndale House Foundation. Used by permission of Tyndale House Publishers, Carol Stream, Illinois 60188. All rights reserved.